T0146965

An Analysis of

C. S. Lewis's

Mere Christianity

Mark W. Scarlata

Published by Macat International Ltd
24:13 Coda Centre, 189 Munster Road, London SW6 6AW.

Distributed exclusively by Routledge
2 Park Square, Milton Park, Abingdon, Oxon OX14 4RN
711 Third Avenue, New York, NY 10017, USA

Routledge is an imprint of the Taylor & Francis Group, an informa business

Copyright © 2017 by Macat International Ltd
Macat International has asserted its right under the Copyright, Designs and Patents Act
1988 to be identified as the copyright holder of this work.

The print publication is protected by copyright. Prior to any prohibited reproduction, storage in
a retrieval system, distribution or transmission in any form or by any means, electronic, me-
chanical, recording or otherwise, permission should be obtained from the publisher or where
applicable a license permitting restricted copying in the United Kingdom should be obtained
from the Copyright Licensing Agency Ltd, Barnard's Inn, 86 Fetter Lane, London EC4A 1EN, UK.

The ePublication is protected by copyright and must not be copied, reproduced, transferred,
distributed, leased, licensed or publicly performed or used in any way except as specifically
permitted in writing by the publishers, as allowed under the terms and conditions under which
it was purchased, or as strictly permitted by applicable copyright law. Any unauthorised distribution or use of this text may be a direct infringement of the authors and the publishers' rights
and those responsible may be liable in law accordingly.

www.macat.com
info@macat.com

Cataloguing in Publication Data
A catalogue record for this book is available from the British Library.
Library of Congress Cataloguing-in-Publication Data is available upon request.
Cover illustration: Kim Thompson

ISBN 978-1-912303-86-1 (hardback)
ISBN 978-1-912128-64-8 (paperback)
ISBN 978-1-912282-74-6 (e-book)

Notice
The information in this book is designed to orientate readers of the work under analysis,
to elucidate and contextualise its key ideas and themes, and to aid in the development
of critical thinking skills. It is not meant to be used, nor should it be used, as a
substitute for original thinking or in place of original writing or research. References and
notes are provided for informational purposes and their presence does not constitute
endorsement of the information or opinions therein. This book is presented solely for
educational purposes. It is sold on the understanding that the publisher is not engaged
to provide any scholarly advice. The publisher has made every effort to ensure that
this book is accurate and up-to-date, but makes no warranties or representations with
regard to the completeness or reliability of the information it contains. The information
and the opinions provided herein are not guaranteed or warranted to produce particular
results and may not be suitable for students of every ability. The publisher shall not be
liable for any loss, damage or disruption arising from any errors or omissions, or from
the use of this book, including, but not limited to, special, incidental, consequential or
other damages caused, or alleged to have been caused, directly or indirectly, by the
information contained within.

CONTENTS

THE MACAT LIBRARY

The Macat Library is a series of unique academic explorations of seminal works in the humanities and social sciences – books and papers that have had a significant and widely recognised impact on their disciplines. It has been created to serve as much more than just a summary of what lies between the covers of a great book. It illuminates and explores the influences on, ideas of, and impact of that book. Our goal is to offer a learning resource that encourages critical thinking and fosters a better, deeper understanding of important ideas.

Each publication is divided into three Sections: Influences, Ideas, and Impact. Each Section has four Modules. These explore every important facet of the work, and the responses to it.

This Section-Module structure makes a Macat Library book easy to use, but it has another important feature. Because each Macat book is written to the same format, it is possible (and encouraged!) to cross-reference multiple Macat books along the same lines of inquiry or research. This allows the reader to open up interesting interdisciplinary pathways.

To further aid your reading, lists of glossary terms and people mentioned are included at the end of this book (these are indicated by an asterisk [*] throughout) – as well as a list of works cited.

Macat has worked with the University of Cambridge to identify the elements of critical thinking and understand the ways in which six different skills combine to enable effective thinking.
Three allow us to fully understand a problem; three more give us the tools to solve it. Together, these six skills make up the **PACIER** model of critical thinking. They are:

ANALYSIS – understanding how an argument is built
EVALUATION – exploring the strengths and weaknesses of an argument
INTERPRETATION – understanding issues of meaning

CREATIVE THINKING – coming up with new ideas and fresh connections
PROBLEM-SOLVING – producing strong solutions
REASONING – creating strong arguments

To find out more, visit **WWW.MACAT.COM.**

CRITICAL THINKING AND *MERE CHRISTIANITY*

Primary critical thinking skill: REASONING
Secondary critical thinking skill: INTERPRETATION

C.S. Lewis's *Mere Christianity* is a perfect example of one of the most effective aspects of critical thinking skills: the use of reasoning to build a strong, logical argument.

Lewis originally wrote the book as a series of radio talks given from 1942-1944, at the height of World War II. The talks were designed to lay out the most basic tenets of Christianity for listeners, and to use these to make a logical argument for Christian belief and Christian ethics. While Lewis was not an academically-trained theologian or philosopher (specializing instead in literature), his own experience of converting from atheism to Christianity, along with his wide reading and incisive questioning, power a charming but persuasive argument for his own beliefs.

Whether or not one agrees with Lewis's arguments or shares his faith, *Mere Christianity* exemplifies one of the most useful aspects of good reasoning: accessibility. When using reasoning to construct a convincing argument, it is crucial that your audience follow you, and Lewis was a master at constructing well-organised arguments that are immediately understandable to readers. The beautifully written *Mere Christianity* is a masterclass in cogently walking an audience through an elegant and well thought-through piece of reasoning.

ABOUT THE AUTHOR OF THE ORIGINAL WORK

C. S. Lewis was born in 1898 into a religious family from Belfast, Northern Ireland. His mother died when he was nine, after which he was sent to boarding school. By his mid-teens Lewis had become an atheist, and it wasn't until 1929, when he was working as an academic at Oxford University, that Lewis converted to Christianity. He spent the rest of his life exploring his faith: becoming a professor at Cambridge University, a bestselling children's author, and an internationally renowned defender of Christianity. C. S. Lewis died in 1963 at the age of 64.

ABOUT THE AUTHOR OF THE ANALYSIS

The Reverend **Dr Mark Scarlata** is Vicar-Chaplain at the church of St Edward King and Martyr, Cambridge. He holds a PhD in Old Testament studies from the University of Cambridge and is senior lecturer at St Mellitus Theological College in London. The Revd Dr Scarlata is the author of *'Am I My Brother's Keeper?': Christian Citizenship in a Globalized Society* (Cascade Books, 2013).

ABOUT MACAT

GREAT WORKS FOR CRITICAL THINKING

Macat is focused on making the ideas of the world's great thinkers accessible and comprehensible to everybody, everywhere, in ways that promote the development of enhanced critical thinking skills.

It works with leading academics from the world's top universities to produce new analyses that focus on the ideas and the impact of the most influential works ever written across a wide variety of academic disciplines. Each of the works that sit at the heart of its growing library is an enduring example of great thinking. But by setting them in context – and looking at the influences that shaped their authors, as well as the responses they provoked – Macat encourages readers to look at these classics and game-changers with fresh eyes. Readers learn to think, engage and challenge their ideas, rather than simply accepting them.

'Macat offers an amazing first-of-its-kind tool for interdisciplinary learning and research. Its focus on works that transformed their disciplines and its rigorous approach, drawing on the world's leading experts and educational institutions, opens up a world-class education to anyone.'

Andreas Schleicher
Director for Education and Skills, Organisation for Economic Co-operation and Development

'Macat is taking on some of the major challenges in university education ... They have drawn together a strong team of active academics who are producing teaching materials that are novel in the breadth of their approach.'

Prof Lord Broers,
former Vice-Chancellor of the University of Cambridge

'The Macat vision is exceptionally exciting. It focuses upon new modes of learning which analyse and explain seminal texts which have profoundly influenced world thinking and so social and economic development. It promotes the kind of critical thinking which is essential for any society and economy. This is the learning of the future.'

Rt Hon Charles Clarke, former UK Secretary of State for Education

'The Macat analyses provide immediate access to the critical conversation surrounding the books that have shaped their respective discipline, which will make them an invaluable resource to all of those, students and teachers, working in the field.'

Professor William Tronzo, University of California at San Diego

WAYS IN TO THE TEXT

KEY POINTS

- C. S. Lewis is one of the most influential Christian thinkers of the twentieth century. His work makes complex theology*—the systematic study of the nature of God— understandable to everyday readers.

- *Mere Christianity* draws on Lewis's own journey from atheism to faith. Using a simple, straightforward style, the text explains the basic doctrines* of the Christian religion.

- *Mere Christianity* is a groundbreaking text. It was written at a time when the value of faith and the role of the Church in society was being increasingly sidelined in Britain. Yet Lewis, an "amateur" theologian, brought the fundamentals of Christian doctrine to life.

Who Was C. S. Lewis?

C. S. Lewis, the author of *Mere Christianity* (1952), was a well-educated Oxford scholar who later became the professor of medieval* and Renaissance* literature at Cambridge University. He wrote extensively, not only in the academic field of literature, but also as an amateur theologian and as a children's author.

Lewis's extraordinary imagination and readable writing style meant that some of his fictional works—notably the seven children's books that make up *The Chronicles of Narnia*—have enjoyed worldwide success. His theological works have also won widespread admiration. Lewis was an atheist* before his conversion to Christianity, after which he spent his life as a member of the Church of England (the Anglican* Church) and felt the need to explain the doctrines of Christian belief. He wanted to do so with clarity and simplicity, using language that would appeal to the average person.

Lewis's writing covers a wide variety of Christian topics. Some are works that set out to defend the Christian faith, a form of writing known as "apologetics."* In these, Lewis uses a range of philosophical and theological arguments to assert that God exists and to confirm the claims of the Christian faith. He had two distinct strengths that helped him communicate his ideas to a wide audience. One was his ability to break down complex theological arguments. The other was the way he uses illustrations and stories to illuminate his ideas. Lewis was one of those rare scholars who have the ability to communicate to the academic elite as well as to a popular audience. This shines through his writings on the Christian faith and in his popular books of fiction alike.

What Does *Mere Christianity* Say?

C. S. Lewis's book *Mere Christianity* emerged from a series of three radio talks, written and voiced by Lewis for the BBC.* They were broadcast during World War II* and aimed to provide basic explanations of Christian belief on various religious topics. When Lewis converted these broadcasts into book form, he retained their original conversational style and tone. This accessible style is one of the reasons why *Mere Christianity* became one of the classic Christian apologetic texts of the twenty-first century. Its title comes from a phrase that was coined by the English Protestant* theologian Richard Baxter (1615–91). Protestantism is, with Roman Catholicism, one of the two major branches of the Christian faith. But when Baxter talks about "mere Christianity," he is referring to ancient, fundamental beliefs that are common to all Christians. By using this title Lewis hoped to make it clear that his work aims to describe the most basic doctrines of the Christian faith.

Lewis was born into a Protestant family, but early life experiences (including the death of his mother just before his tenth birthday) led him to become an atheist in his teens. He converted to Christianity in 1929, having become convinced of the existence of God. He begins *Mere Christianity* by arguing that it is rational to have a religious belief. From the start of the book, Lewis argues that there is a universal moral law that governs human nature. This moral law tells us what we *ought* to do. Lewis say that the human ability to reason allows us to make a rational claim for the existence of this moral law, despite the fact that it cannot be proved through scientific inquiry. He goes on to say that the existence of this law also leads to the rational conclusion that there is something that exists beyond the material world. This "something" brought all things into existence. It is, in other words, God.

Lewis begins his discussion of "moral law" (the values that govern human behavior) by giving us principles of right and wrong. Although these vary from culture to culture, Lewis argues that there are basic principles, such as prohibitions of killing, stealing, and lying, that are universal. He then asks where these innate moral principles come from. Lewis argues that these values have not simply evolved. Instead, he sees them as reflecting the fact that there is a divine, moral being that exists beyond the material world. These basic universal principles guide human beings about how to function in the world, both in relation to God and to one another.

Having established his reasons for belief in a divine being and moral law, Lewis goes on to explain Christian doctrine. He looks at how Christianity differs from other religions and from philosophies like theism* (the belief in a creator who is not necessarily the Christian God) or pantheism* (the belief that the whole universe is God). Lewis argues that the heart of Christian belief lies in human relationships, the interior moral life, and the end goal of life in relationship with God.

He explores issues such as the cardinal virtues (prudence, temperance, justice, and fortitude) and argues that they are critical for bringing us closer to God. In the final portion of the book, Lewis addresses more complex Christian doctrines. Throughout *Mere Christianity*, Lewis utilizes his vivid imagination to present religious concepts with vitality and life.

Why Does *Mere Christianity* Matter?

Mere Christianity is one of the most widely read apologetics (defenses) of Christianity written in the twentieth century. Not everyone agrees with all of Lewis's beliefs; although some theologians and philosophers dismissed his arguments, *Mere Christianity* was not written for an academic or an ordained audience. Lewis was writing about the fundamentals of his faith, for everyone.

He succeeded in reaching a large lay audience. He also succeeded in producing a defense of the basics of Christianity that revealed the underlying unity of the faith, and its historical and biblical origins.

At the time *Mere Christianity* was published, Western culture was becoming increasing secular.* The wider Western community had lost interest in the Church. Yet Lewis's ideas engaged and refreshed Christians and non-Christians alike; they continue to do so.

The book still matters, both within Christian discourse and in the public arena, because Lewis sought to illuminate the issues that lie at the heart of Christianity. He brought together logic, humor, metaphor, imagination, and myth to an exploration of the essence of faith. Some criticize *Mere Christianity* for avoiding issues that are controversial within the Church. These issues include matters of worship, such as participating in the Eucharist:* celebrating Jesus' death and resurrection through a communion meal of bread and wine. Lewis, however, argues that these controversies make it harder for non-believers to engage with Christianity. His aim is to bring clarity to faith.

The same desire is evident in Lewis's attempts to explain certain theological doctrines and make their meaning plain. He was not always successful, and he certainly had his critics, but his work was not in vain. Lewis's ability to maintain his focus on his core topic—God and core Christian doctrines—is part of the reason *Mere Christianity* was so well received and why it continues to be relevant today.

SECTION 1
INFLUENCES

MODULE 1
THE AUTHOR AND THE HISTORICAL CONTEXT

KEY POINTS

- *Mere Christianity* is one of the most important works of apologetics*—defenses—of the Christian faith written in the twentieth century.

- The book fulfilled a need for an explanation of the Christian faith that spoke to a generation marked by war, scientific advances, and the rise of secularism*—life conducted on non-religious principles.

- Lewis called himself a "reluctant convert" to Christianity.

Why Read This Text?

C. S. Lewis's *Mere Christianity* (1952) is one of the most influential books ever written defending the Christian faith. In 2000, the magazine *Christianity Today* listed the most important books of the twentieth century. *Mere Christianity* came top, described as "the best case for the essentials of orthodox* Christianity in print."[1] The book has been of enduring significance for the Christian faith and Church since its publication.

Lewis wrote the book for an audience that no longer valued the usefulness of religion. It was an amalgamation of three radio talks on the Christian faith he gave on the British Broadcasting Corporation (BBC)* between 1942 and 1944. These radio talks were originally published as three separate transcripts, in pamphlets titled "The Case for Christianity" (1942), "Christian Behaviour" (1943), and "Beyond Personality" (1944). The intellectual climate of the mid-twentieth century was one of modernization and change; this affected politics,

> 66 We were coming, my brother and I, to rely more and more exclusively on each other for all that made life bearable; to have confidence only in each other. I expect that we (or at any rate I) were already learning to lie to him. Everything that had made the house a home had failed us; everything except one another. We drew closer together (that was the good result)— two frightened urchins huddled for warmth in a bleak world. 99
>
> C. S. Lewis, *Surprised by Joy: The Shape of My Early Life.*

the arts, science, and society and contributed to a move away from general religious belief to a trust in human progress and modernity. Furthermore, Britain was then engaged in World War II:* Lewis addressed a world in crisis.

In these uncertain times, Lewis reached into the heart of the Christian faith, setting out to explain its basics. In a world that was questioning the bedrocks of Christian faith, he communicated a clear and accessible understanding of the value of Christianity. The straightforward logic and clarity of *Mere Christianity* are its greatest gifts, and they helped make the work the most popular defense of Christianity of the twentieth century.

Author's Life

Clive Staples Lewis was born in Belfast (now in Northern Ireland) in November 1898. His seemingly idyllic childhood ended with his mother's death from cancer. Lewis was nine years old. The loss devastated him. In his autobiography, *Surprised by Joy: The Shape of My Early Life* (1955), he describes his mother's death as his "first religious experience." He thought that in her illness "his prayers for her recovery would be successful."[2] When she died, he felt God had failed him by not answering these prayers.

Lewis's biographer Colin Duriez has speculated that Lewis's grief drew him closer to his brother, but separated him from his father. His father could not express his own grief and sent the young Lewis to boarding school,[3] where he struggled socially. It was at school that he ultimately abandoned his faith and became an atheist.* This lack of belief in God was later strengthened by a private tutor, the atheist and logician W. T. Kirkpatrick,* who taught Lewis to think critically and speak purposefully.

Lewis went on to study classics, philosophy, and ancient history at Oxford University. In 1917, however, he left his studies to enlist in the military and was deployed to France to fight in World War I.* After the war ended, Lewis returned to Oxford to complete his studies and took up a teaching position at Magdalene College in 1925. He stayed at Oxford for 29 years before accepting a professorship in medieval and Renaissance* literature at Cambridge University. It was during his time at Cambridge that Lewis married the American writer Joy Davidman.* They were married for only four years before she died from cancer in 1960. Three years later, Lewis himself died.

Author's Background

Lewis's private tutor, W. T. Kirkpatrick, had a profound influence on him. Lewis recalls one of his first meetings with Kirkpatrick, during which the tutor criticized Lewis's casual use of the word "wildness" to describe their surroundings. Kirkpatrick proceeded to lecture Lewis on the logic—or illogic—of his statement. Lewis writes that "the tone set by this first conversation was preserved without a single break during all the years I spent at Bookham."[4] This dedication to the discipline of logic would become the backbone of *Mere Christianity*.

Lewis was also influenced by his exposure to English literature, the classics, philosophy, and the Nordic mythologies (the myth of pre-

Christian Scandinavia) that he studied at Oxford. Yet, despite the secular influences that surrounded Lewis at university, in 1929 he wrote that he finally admitted that God was God. He labeled himself "the most dejected and reluctant convert in all of England."[5] But his newfound faith helped shape the future of his writing career. Alongside his scholarly works in English literature, Lewis wanted to address the assumption that Christianity was somehow obsolete. This led to him writing a series of radio pieces that would later form the basis of *Mere Christianity*. These were influenced by Lewis's intellectual background—he was well trained in philosophical and rational thought—as well as by his love for myth and imagination. While many of the key ideas were not original, Lewis's clear explanation and defense of these ideas made his text distinctive.

NOTES

1   David S. Dockery, "Books of the Century," *Christianity Today*, April 24, 2000, accessed September 8, 2015, http://www.christianitytoday.com/ct/2000/april24/5.92.html.

2   C. S. Lewis, *Surprised by Joy: The Shape of My Early Life* (New York: Harcourt Brace, 1955), 20.

3   Colin Duriez, *The A–Z of C. S. Lewis: An Encyclopaedia of His Life, Thought, and Writings* (Oxford: Lion Hudson, 2013), 167.

4   Lewis, *Surprised by Joy*, 135.

5   Lewis, *Surprised by Joy*, 13–15.

MODULE 2
ACADEMIC CONTEXT

KEY POINTS

- Lewis defended Christianity against liberal theologians who sought to break down and reinterpret Christian belief in order to demythologize* it—that is, to explain Christianity in historical rather than mythological terms.

- Lewis argued that Jesus could not be seen simply as a moral teacher.

- Lewis's colleagues and friends at Oxford had a significant influence on his thinking and conversion to Christianity.

The Work in its Context

When C. S. Lewis's book *Mere Christianity* was published in 1952, the prevailing intellectual culture was one that valued objective, scientific proofs. Ever since the late seventeenth century and the period of intellectual history known as the Enlightenment,* Western thinking had moved away from supernatural explanations of the world. People no longer believed in things like miracles. As a result, from the 1930s to the 1950s, liberal theologians, who denied the historicity of much of the writing inherited by the Christian tradition, argued that Christianity had to be deconstructed and demythologized if it were to survive in the modern world. As Lewis writes, "It follows that, to them, the most mischievous people in the world are those who, like myself, proclaim that Christianity essentially involves the supernatural. They are quite sure that belief in the supernatural never will, nor should, be revived, and that if we convince the world that it must choose between accepting the supernatural and abandoning all pretense of Christianity, the world will undoubtedly choose the second alternative."[1]

> ❝ I hope no reader will suppose that 'mere' Christianity is here put forward as an alternative to the creeds of the existing communions. ❞
>
> C. S. Lewis, *Mere Christianity*

Lewis understood liberal theology* (the study of the nature of God) as an effort to undermine Christian orthodoxy.* *Mere Christianity* was, in essence, his defense of the traditional Christian faith in a secular forum. One of his main aims was to provide a guide to core Christian beliefs that were common across denominations* (sects) and that had been part of Christian belief since the Church began: "For I am not writing to expound something I could call 'my religion', but to expound 'mere' Christianity, which is what it is and what it was long before I was born and whether I like it or not."[2] Lewis wants to look beyond the details of theological controversies. His intention is to offer a simple, logical presentation of the Christian faith that emphasizes the unity of Christian heritage.

Overview of the Field

While Lewis set out to defend the basics of Christianity rather than to convert anyone to his particular beliefs, he was writing at a time when particular trends were certainly shaping Christian theology. One of the most influential thinkers of the time was the German biblical scholar Rudolf Bultmann,* an advocate of methodological naturalism. Methodological naturalism is the belief that what we know about the natural world can only come through scientific observation and testing. For Bultmann, supernatural events—like miracles—could not exist because they do not conform to scientific studies founded on evidence verifiable by observation, which search for natural causes to explain natural phenomena. In texts such as *New Testament and Mythology* (1941), Bultmann calls for the biblical texts to be demythologized: stripped of spirits and miracles. He argues that this would free the Christian faith from its mythological leanings.

Lewis argued against this type of "demythologized" Christianity. Although Lewis was not a theologian in the academic sense, his work provides a defense of the miraculous. Naturalists such as Bultmann sought to read the Bible from a strictly empirical viewpoint, seeing Jesus as a moral leader. Lewis addresses this by asking "is not the popular idea of Christianity simply this: that Jesus Christ was a great moral teacher and that if only we took His advice we might be able to establish a better social order and avoid another war?"[3] But he rejects it: "If Christianity only means one more bit of good advice, then Christianity is of no importance."[4] Instead, Lewis argues that the doctrine* of Christian faith rests firmly on the claims of Jesus to be the Son of God as well as on the miracle of his death and resurrection. For Lewis, Christianity is not a moralistic religion with Jesus as the great moral teacher: it is a faith that relies on supernatural events.

Academic Influences

At Oxford, Lewis was influenced by the British philosopher Owen Barfield,* who he identified as his chief critic. Barfield accused him of "chronological snobbery" or "the uncritical acceptance of the intellectual climate common to our own age and the assumption that whatever has gone out of date is on that account discredited."[5] This insight led Lewis to question his initial philosophical position as a "realist"—someone who believed that the fundamental realities of the universe are revealed by the senses. Another colleague was the Anglo-Saxon literature scholar and fantasy writer J. R. R. Tolkien,* a fellow Christian. He helped Lewis understand Christianity as a story about God entering history and, along with Barfield, was a member of Lewis's Oxford literary discussion group the Inklings. These men played a significant role in Lewis's formation as a scholar and in guiding him toward the Christian faith.

The Scottish author George MacDonald* also influenced Lewis in his love for myth and story. Lewis describes how MacDonald's fantasy novel *Phantastes* (1858) opened him up, at the age of 16, to the notion of holiness: "That night my imagination was, in a certain sense, baptized; the rest of me, not unnaturally, took longer."[6] In reading *Phantastes*, Lewis felt that his former erotic and mythological imagination had gone through some sort of change. This transformation was another step toward his conversion to Christianity.

NOTES

1   C. S. Lewis, *Letters to Malcomb: Chiefly on Prayer* (San Diego: Harcourt Brace, 1964), 119.

2   C. S. Lewis, *Mere Christianity*, 50th edn (London: HarperCollins, 2001), vii.

3   Lewis, *Mere Christianity*,156.

4   Lewis, *Mere Christianity*, 156.

5   Lewis, *Mere Christianity*, 207–8.

6   Lewis, *Mere Christianity*, 181.

MODULE 3
THE PROBLEM

KEY POINTS

- Lewis set out to write a logical defense for a belief in God and the doctrines* of the Christian faith.

- Lewis took part in a famous debate about naturalism* (the belief that we can only understand the world through scientific observation) and reason with the British philosopher Elizabeth Anscombe* in 1948.

- As a result of the debate, Lewis revised his position on naturalism. However, he never abandoned the belief that there were some things that could not be explained by natural causation.

Core Question

Having converted from atheism, C. S. Lewis's main concern in his book *Mere Christianity* is to establish a logical argument for religious belief. To do this, Lewis challenges the philosophy of naturalism.

Naturalism argues that everything that exists arises as the product of natural causes. A fundamental argument of naturalism is that the "supernatural" does not exist: so any phenomenon that appears supernatural is either false, or can ultimately be explained through naturally occurring causes. For naturalists, the world and everything in it is self-contained and self-originating. It does not rely on anything outside of itself.

In his book *Miracles* (1947), and again in *Mere Christianity,* Lewis attacks the naturalist position. He argues that naturalism is implausible or illogical. How can reason be produced solely by natural causes in the physical world? Lewis says that one's thoughts are not "rational" if

> ❝ I know that some people say the idea of a Law of Nature or decent behavior known to all men is unsound, because different civilizations and different ages have had quite different moralities. But this is not true. There have been differences between their moralities, but these have never amounted to anything like a total difference. ❞
>
> C. S. Lewis, *Mere Christianity*

those thoughts are merely determined by unfolding events. This leaves no room for rational inference—the human logic and rational thinking that underpins naturalism itself. Lewis argues that if the logic of naturalism is applied to naturalism itself, naturalists would have to end up rejecting its precepts: "Even if grounds do exist [for accepting that thoughts are produced through natural causes], what have they got to do with the actual occurrence of belief as a psychological event? If it is an event it must be caused. It must in fact be simply one link in a causal chain that stretched back to the beginning and forward to the end of time. How could such a trifle as lack of logical grounds prevent the belief's occurrence and how could the existence of grounds promote it?"[1]

The Participants

Lewis did not direct his apologetic*—defense—for Christianity at any particular scholar. He did, however, engage with different philosophers and theologians throughout his career. One of his most famous debates was with the British philosopher Elizabeth Anscombe at the Oxford Socratic Club*—a debating society where religious topics were discussed. This took place in 1948, four years before the publication of *Mere Christianity*. In the debate, Anscombe replied to one of Lewis's argument in *Miracles*, in which Lewis argued that if naturalism were accepted, it meant that rational thought could only occur through irrational causes. Anscombe argued that Lewis needed to make a distinction between something being irrational (flawed) and non-rational (not derived from rational thought). As an example, Darwinism*—evolutionary* theory founded on the work of the British naturalist Charles Darwin*—may occur through non-rational causes. Anscombe suggested that if Lewis made this distinction, he would be able to accept that rational thought can be the product of natural and non-rational causes.

Lewis's arguments also touch on Darwinism. Darwinists use science to explain the world, showing that the natural world could be explained in its entirety as the result of physics and chemistry. In his attack on naturalism, Lewis argued that naturalists would reject Darwinism, because they would not be able to trust the scientific reasoning behind this explanation of the world. Lewis's point is that if a materialist* says she believes in something because she recognizes a reason for believing it, she must therefore believe in the existence of reason.

The Contemporary Debate

Although most believe that Anscombe won the debate, some critics have recently suggested that it would be fairer to see it as a draw.[2] What is indisputable is that the debate convinced Lewis to soften his argument against naturalism.

Even so, he continued to defend his rationalistic* position in *Mere Christianity*, arguing that human beings reach true conclusions through reason. Reason, he says, is best understood through theistic metaphysics*—the belief that God exists beyond our natural experience. He argues for theistic metaphysics in place of naturalistic metaphysics* (the belief that nothing exists beyond the natural world).

This argument is critical in the early chapters of *Mere Christianity*, providing the foundation of Lewis's argument that it is rational to believe in God and moral law. Lewis's argument would never satisfy a real naturalist because he does not abandon the connection he draws between natural causes and unnatural causes to aspects of material existence. Although Anscombe helped him refine his thinking, Lewis maintained that there is something that exists that is not nature—and this *something* cannot be explained. If it could be, there would have been nothing to debate or rationalize.

No clear consensus was reached between Lewis and his naturalist opponents. The debate still continues today.

NOTES

1   C. S. Lewis, *Miracles: A Preliminary Study* (New York: Macmillan, 1960), 16.

2   See, for instance, John Owens, "C. S. Lewis's Argument against Naturalism," in *A Myth Retold: Re-Encountering C. S. Lewis as Theologian*, ed. Martin Sutherland (Eugene, OR: Wipf and Stock, 2014), 57–9; Victor Reppert, C. S. Lewis's Dangerous Idea: In Defense of the Argument of Reason (Downers Grove, IL: InterVarsity Press, 2003).

MODULE 4
THE AUTHOR'S CONTRIBUTION

KEY POINTS

- Lewis offers a clear explanation and defense of the most basic tenets of Christian belief—a "mere" Christianity.

- Lewis's chief contribution lay in his style, not in his theology.* He was able to clarify complex debates and make his faith readily accessible to lay people.

- Lewis's popularity as an academic and author of fictional books helped to enrich his defense of the Christian faith.

Author's Aims

C. S. Lewis's primary objective in *Mere Christianity* is to offer a coherent account of religious belief in a world where religion is being sidelined. At the time when he was writing, competing accounts of human existence were questioning the validity of religion and the moral or ethical laws that govern humanity. Lewis does not (necessarily) set out to evangelize or convert others to Christian doctrine, but rather to present a plausible argument: first, that Christianity is true, and, second, because Christianity is true, it must be reckoned with in the public forum.

Unlike most theological arguments, Lewis was not directing his core ideas at any particular scholarly position. Instead, he addresses a British society whom he believes has reduced religion to the level of personal experience rather than seeing it as having a universal claim on all humanity. *Mere Christianity*, at its core, is less about addressing a particular theology and more concerned about correcting what Lewis perceives as a misrepresentation of the Christian faith in general society.

> 66 With his pen and with his voice on the radio Mr Lewis has succeeded in capturing the attention of many who will not readily listen to professional theologians, and has taught them many lessons concerning the deep things of God. 99
>
> D. M. Baillie, at the ceremony for C. S. Lewis's honorary Doctorate of Divinity, June 28, 1946, University of St Andrews

In the preface to *Mere Christianity*, Lewis emphasizes that he is not setting out to make any distinctions between different Christian denominations* such as Protestant* or Roman Catholic* or expounding on their particular doctrines. Instead, he is undertaking a defense of Christian beliefs that have been common to nearly all Christians at all times: "For I am not writing to expound something I could call 'my religion', but to expound 'mere' Christianity, which is what it is and what it was long before I was born and whether I like it or not."[1]

His aim is to present an account of historic Christianity that centers on orthodox* beliefs still held in common despite centuries of doctrinal division.

Approach

Lewis's text stands out for its author's ability to use common language to communicate his arguments. Unlike academic theologians or philosophers, who used highly technical language and complex arguments, Lewis wrote as a layperson to other laypeople. His style was simple, yet intellectually challenging. In an essay on apologetics,* Lewis writes, "Our business is to present that which is timeless (the same yesterday, today, and tomorrow) in the particular language of our own age."[2] He viewed his task as that of a translator: taking Christian doctrine and putting it into the vernacular of a lay audience. The original goal, then, of *Mere Christianity* in its original form of lectures given on BBC* radio, and later as a written publication, was not to appeal to other theologians or philosophers but to speak to the average person. To do this, Lewis uses a speaking and writing style that employs plain analogies and metaphors. These could be grasped easily by anyone with any level of education.

Lewis's desire to engage the non-Christian and the non-theologian (that is, those who are not expert in Christian doctrine through the analysis of Scripture) is central to his task of explaining what "mere" Christianity means. Although Lewis often uses sophisticated arguments, his language is simple and straightforward. And whether among university professors or in front of factory workers, Lewis argues for a rational belief in God and the logical consistency of the Christian faith.

Contribution in Context

Lewis was not putting forward an original defense of Christian belief. In 1908, 44 years before Lewis published *Mere Christianity*, the English writer and then Anglican* G. K. Chesterton* had put forward very similar arguments in his book *Orthodoxy*. Although Chesterton influenced Lewis,[3] their books focused on different sources as starting points for their discussion about the essence of Christianity. Chesterton looked to the Apostles' Creed, an early statement of Christian belief, supposedly drawn from the teachings of the 12 chief disciples of Jesus. In contrast, Lewis turned to the *Book of Common Prayer*, the service book of the Anglican Church, first printed in 1549.

Lewis was convinced that humanity's destiny was to experience unfettered joy in relationship with a supreme and unsurpassable God. He discusses the way that Christian principles can help people achieve this. Within this, he looks at moral behavior and how to live the virtuous life. His exploration of morality draws on his earlier training in philosophy—his thinking is influenced by the work of the ancient Greek philosophers Plato* and Aristotle*—and from his work in medieval* and Renaissance* literature. Lewis takes a distinctly premodern* stance when he describes moral behavior as something that arises from, and reinforces, character. Secular* thought of his day—thought founded on non-religious principles—tended to isolate experiences and decisions. But Lewis saw moral choices as building blocks that led to character development and the virtuous life.

The key contribution that Lewis makes in *Mere Christianity* is his ability to express Christian doctrine at both a scholarly and an imaginative level. Part of what makes Lewis's work so compelling and unique is that his theology* filters through his popular children's fiction work *The Chronicles of Narnia* as well as his other fictional works. Lewis's prolific writing career brought to life many of the ideas found in *Mere Christianity*.

NOTES

1   C. S. Lewis, *Mere Christianity*, 50th edn (London: HarperCollins, 2001), vii.

2   C. S. Lewis, "Christian Apologetics," in *God in the Dock: Essays on Theology and Ethics* (Grand Rapids, MI: Eerdmans, 1970), 89–103.

3   See Richard L. Purtill, *C. S. Lewis' Case for the Christian Faith* (San Francisco: Ignatius, 2004), 175.

SECTION 2
IDEAS

MAIN IDEAS

KEY POINTS

- One of the main ideas in *Mere Christianity* is that there is a universal moral law common to all humanity.

- Lewis argues against the popular philosophy of materialism* (according to which all facts about humanity depend on physical processes). He contends that there is more to life than can be studied in the natural world.

- Lewis's direct language and imaginative analogies helped the text appeal to a large and diverse readership.

Key Themes

The main themes of C. S. Lewis's *Mere Christianity* are: the defense of the Christian faith and a universal moral law; the criticism of naturalism* (the belief that we can only understand the world through scientific observation) and materialism* (the belief that the only thing that exists is matter, which is accessed through one's senses); and the move away from secular* beliefs in modern society.

Mere Christianity is divided into four books. The first addresses what Lewis calls "the law of human nature." In it, he argues, first, that there is a moral law that governs human life, and, second, that people know when they have broken that law. In Book 2, Lewis moves on to Christian belief, discussing the distinction between those who believe in a god and those that do not. Book 3 is dedicated to Christian behavior. Here, Lewis describes moral laws as directions for running the human machine. Rather than seeing morality as a restriction on humanity coming from God, Lewis argues that it should be seen as a way to improve the human experience.

> **❝** In religion, as in war and everything else, comfort is the one thing you cannot get by looking for it. If you look for truth, you may find comfort in the end: if you look for comfort you will not get either comfort or truth—only soft soap and wishful thinking to begin with and, in the end, despair. **❞**
>
> C. S. Lewis, *Mere Christianity*

He discusses three aspects of morality: human relationships; the interior moral life; and the end goal of life in relationship with God.

In the final book, Lewis moves into deeper theological themes. He touches on an understanding of God as three persons in one form—the Christian concept of the Trinity* of the Father, the Son, and the Holy Spirit.* He also discusses God's relationship to space and time. His conclusion is that the Christian life is not about personal improvement but about our human potential to transform into the image of Christ. Lewis argues that each decision we make either conforms us to God's desires or turns us further away from them.

Exploring the Ideas

Mere Christianity begins with a logical defense (known as an apologetic*) for the existence of God and a universal moral law (or natural law). This was Lewis's response to society's move away from traditional religious beliefs toward a secular and materialist view of the world. While the laws of nature are understood through the study of observable facts, Lewis contends that natural law reveals that there is something beyond this—and this points to a universal moral law that governs our notion of how humans should behave. Lewis says there must be something behind morality, which is directing the universe and "appears in me as a law urging me to do right and making me feel responsible and uncomfortable when I do wrong."[1]

He does not argue for the existence of the Christian God. Instead he simply observes that if a moral law exists, life cannot be confined to a material reality.

Lewis argues against the popular philosophy of materialism. In its most basic form, materialism says the only thing that exists is matter, which we discover and understand through sensory experience. Lewis asks his readers to take seriously the idea that this is not all there is to life, writing, "It is after you have realized that there is a real Moral Law, and a Power behind the law, and that you have broken that law and put yourself wrong with that Power—it is after all this, and not a moment sooner, that Christianity begins to talk. When you know you are sick, you will listen to the doctor."[2]

Language and Expression

Mere Christianity began as three separate radio broadcasts: *Broadcast Talks* (1942), *Christian Behaviour* (1943), and *Beyond Personality* (1944). The book's origins in radio helped give the text its distinctive tone: clear, conversational, and direct. It is because of its simplicity of expression that *Mere Christianity* is so effective as an apologetic. Lewis uses simple analogies to explain difficult concepts. Instead of abstract terms, he uses concrete images to convey his points. For example, in his preface he compares "mere" Christianity to a great hall out of which doors open into various rooms. His intent in the book is to invite people into the hall, which represents the simplest elements of Christian doctrine. Readers must choose which room to enter, but Lewis encourages the reader to "be kind to those who have chosen different doors and to those who are still in the hall. If they are wrong they need your prayers all the more; and if they are your enemies, then you are under orders to pray for them. That is one of the rules common to the whole house."[3]

Lewis also employed simple illustrations to communicate his ideas, such as his famous "Liar, Lunatic, or Lord" argument in the chapter

"The Shocking Alternative." Here, he states the choices one has when confronted with the claims made by Christ: "I am trying here to prevent anyone saying the really foolish thing that people often say about Him: 'I'm ready to accept Jesus as a great moral teacher, but I don't accept His claim to be God.' That is the one thing we must not say. A man who was merely a man and said the sort of things Jesus said would not be a great moral teacher. He would either be a lunatic—on a level with the man who says he is a poached egg—or else he would be the Devil of Hell."[4]

Lewis was not trying to convert anyone to his position. He was trying to shed light on contemporary beliefs about Jesus to demonstrate that they were untenable. Neither was he taking unique or original positions in his defense of Christianity. He wanted to establish rational arguments that could be understood by a non-academic audience. *Mere Christianity* was written to speak to people from every walk of life.

NOTES

1   C. S. Lewis, *Mere Christianity*, 50th edn (London: HarperCollins, 2001), 25.

2   Lewis, *Mere Christianity*, 31–2.

3   Lewis, *Mere Christianity*, xiv.

4   Lewis, *Mere Christianity*, 55.

MODULE 6
SECONDARY IDEAS

KEY POINTS

- Lewis establishes a distinction between biological and spiritual life. He argues that by looking outside ourselves, away from our material concerns, we find the key to the transformative journey that leads to God.

- Lewis saw "prudence" as the most important of the four "cardinal virtues" (prudence, temperance, justice, and fortitude) that underpin his moral theory.

- Although Lewis was best known for his children's fantasy novels and his apologetics,* it is through looking at his whole body of work that we understand the full range of his ideas.

Other Ideas

One of the key secondary ideas in C. S. Lewis's *Mere Christianity* is the distinction between the biblical Greek words *Bios* and *Zoe*. In English bibles, both are translated as "life"—but for Lewis they mean totally different things: while *Bios* is biological life, *Zoe* is spiritual life. Lewis proposes that in our natural condition, human beings have a self-centered biological life, but not necessarily a developed connection to the spiritual world. And while our natural life is inward looking, the spiritual looks outward to a world, which, if we choose to engage with it, will transform us as human beings. Lewis likens this process to people who are brought up to be dirty and are afraid to wash. The selfish *Bios* resists bathing in the knowledge that once you are washed you will be transformed. Lewis suggests that it is this transformation, the turn to spirituality or *Zoe,* which ultimately lets people resemble God.

> 66 Morality, then, seems to be concerned with three things. Firstly, with fair play and harmony between individuals. Secondly, with what might be called tidying up or harmonizing the things inside each individual. Thirdly, with the general purpose of human life as a whole: what man was made for: what course the whole fleet ought to be on: what tune the conductor of the band wants it to play. 99
>
> C. S. Lewis, *Mere Christianity*

In Lewis's time, a popular opinion was that "Jesus Christ was a great moral teacher and that if only we took His advice we might be able to establish a better social order and avoid another war."[1] Lewis responds, "If Christianity only means one more bit of good advice, then Christianity is of no importance."[2] Here Lewis contends that human beings have both a biological life and a spiritual life, and that the spiritual life is transformative. He likens this transformation to a statue of carved stone being changed into a real person, concluding, "This world is a great sculptor's shop. We are the statues and there is a rumor going round the shop that some of us are some day going to come to life."[3] Lewis argues that to approach the Christian faith, people must either accept or reject its claims. But they must not try to water down those claims to make Christianity more palatable.

Exploring the Ideas
The distinction between *Bio* and *Zoe* is, essentially, the distinction between the lives that humans have and the life that God has. Lewis returns frequently to the relationship between morality and theology. In part three of his book he looks at Christian practice and character formation. He discusses the four "cardinal virtues"—prudence, temperance, justice, and fortitude.

Prudence is listed first. This is a critical aspect of Lewis's moral theory. Prudence, as Lewis describes it, is practical common sense. It requires people to utilize their intellect as well as they can. Lewis argues that prudence is strengthened by constant exposure to difficult situations. These require decisions to be made that will either strengthen one's morality or diminish it. As such, prudence is vital for a life of virtue.

Lewis believes that Christian morality is a process of inner transformation that depends on every choice a person makes. He argues against the type of morality that sees God as the cosmic lawgiver, rewarding good deeds and punishing bad deeds. Instead, he writes, "I would much rather say that every time you make a choice you are turning the central part of you, the part of you that chooses, into something a little different from what it was before. And taking your life as a whole, with all your innumerable choices, all your life long you are slowly turning this central thing either into a heavenly creature or into a hellish creature: either into a creature that is in harmony with God, and with other creatures, and with itself, or else into one that is in a state of war and hatred with God, and with its fellow creatures, and with itself."[4]

For Lewis, the spiritual life is elevating. It is the transformation from a human creature into the Son of God. The human race exists to be taken to this divine, spiritual life, and if we do not sin in our choices this elevation will occur.

Overlooked

Mere Christianity has received a lot of scholarly attention. As a result it is hard to find any aspects of the book that have been ignored. One area of research that could be explored further, however, is the examination of the text in the light of Lewis's whole corpus. Much attention has been drawn to Lewis's spiritual journey, the success of his fictional writings, and the impact of his apologetics. His public popularity is well known. On September 8, 1947 he was featured on the cover of *Time* magazine as one of the premier fiction writers and lay theologians of his day. But the fact that Lewis spent most of his life in the secluded and sometimes impenetrable world of academia is sometimes overlooked. There, he delivered lectures, gave tutorials to students, and wrote books on medieval* and Renaissance* literature (that is, on literature produced between, roughly, the sixth and the seventeenth centuries). And not much has been written about his scholarly career and its impact on works like *Mere Christianity*. However, much of what makes *Mere Christianity* such a significant work is the way Lewis incorporates so much of his academic learning into his apologetics. His background in literary criticism and the way this informs his readings of biblical texts could be a fertile area of investigation.

NOTES

1   C. S. Lewis, *Mere Christianity*, 50th edn (London: HarperCollins, 2001), 156.

2   Lewis, *Mere Christianity*, 156.

3   Lewis, *Mere Christianity*, 159.

4   Lewis, *Mere Christianity*, 92.

MODULE 7
ACHIEVEMENT

KEY POINTS

* *Mere Christianity* explains the fundamental aspects of Christian doctrine* in a logical and approachable manner.

* Lewis possessed an unusual combination of skills—he was a writer, a thinker, and a literary scholar.

* Lewis was not a trained philosopher or theologian.* This left his arguments open to criticism.

Assessing the Argument

Did C. S. Lewis make a convincing case for Christianity in his book *Mere Christianity*? His goal was to reach a wide readership and to explain and defend the fundamental aspects of the Christian tradition. To achieve this, Lewis did not address potentially controversial topics in the book. These topics included the Virgin Mary*—the mother of Jesus Christ—and particular practices in worship. He acknowledges this, explaining that these are issues that are disputed within the Church, and that he wants to focus on the shared foundations of Christian belief. Before publishing *Mere Christianity*, Lewis sent copies of the book to clergymen of four different Christian denominations*— the Protestant Anglican,* Methodist,* and Presbyterian* denominations, and the Roman Catholic.* While all had their criticisms, each agreed that Lewis had presented the essentials of orthodox* Christian faith.

The continuing popularity of *Mere Christianity* in an increasingly secular* culture is also testimony to its power. As one reviewer from the *Times Literary Supplement* wrote, "Mr. Lewis has a quite unique power of making theology an attractive, exciting and (one might

> **❝** Give up yourself, and you will find your real self. Lose your life and you will save it. Submit to death, death of your ambitions and favorite wishes every day and death of your whole body in the end: submit with every fiber of your being, and you will find eternal life. **❞**
>
> C. S. Lewis, *Mere Christianity*

almost say) an uproariously fascinating quest … Those who have inherited Christianity may write about it with truth and learning, but they can scarcely write with the excitement which men like … C. S. Lewis show, to whom the Christian faith is the unlooked-for discovery of the pearl of great price."[1]

Lewis receives similar plaudits in a more recent publication. In *Indelible Ink* (2003), 22 Christian leaders discuss the books that have made the biggest impact on their lives. Lewis is ranked as the top Christian author, and *Mere Christianity* as the top book.[2] Lewis's skill in presenting clear, logical, and accessible arguments has given his work lasting relevance and turned *Mere Christianity* into one of the most successful apologetics* of the twentieth century.

Achievement in Context

Another factor that may contribute to Lewis's contemporary success as an apologist is the fact that his arguments span a wide range of literary styles. Much of Lewis's body of work contains the Christian themes of faith, sin, sacrifice, rebirth, and transformation. Some of his core ideas are present in his children's books, like the *Chronicles of Narnia* (1950–6), his science fiction, and his other essays and poetry. In *The Lion, the Witch and the Wardrobe* (1950), for example, we find Professor Kirke backing Lucy's claim that she has been to Narnia: "There are only three possibilities. Either your sister is telling lies, or she is mad, or she is telling the truth. You know she doesn't tell lies and it is obvious that she is not mad. For the moment then and unless any further evidence turns up, we must assume that she is telling the truth."[3]

This argument is similar to the argument Lewis makes in *Mere Christianity* in which he talks about the claims made by Jesus. Lewis says that given these claims, there are only three possibilities about Jesus: he is either the Lord, or a liar, or a lunatic.

Other Christian motifs run through *The Lion, the Witch and the Wardrobe*. For example, Aslan the Lion is sacrificed on behalf of Edmund. This redemptive act mirrors the sacrifice of Christ on behalf of the sins of humanity. Aslan undergoes bodily resurrection, which also parallels the Christian story of Christ's resurrection. In *Mere Christianity*, in the chapter entitled "The Shocking Alternative," Lewis discusses the need for Christ's death and resurrection.

With the skill of a literary scholar, the sharpened intellect of a philosopher, and the understanding of a children's author, Lewis made his arguments known in the different genres of his writing. This diversity of approach has added to his recognition and popularity.

Limitations

Yet despite its achievements, it can be argued that *Mere Christianity* did not achieve all of Lewis's goals. It is claimed that some of his arguments do not deal fully with the philosophical and theological complexity of the issues they address. The English academic and Jesuit* priest Peter Milward,* a former pupil of Lewis, notes Lewis's lack of engagement with the figure of the Virgin Mary. For Milward, this causes a problematic contradiction in *Mere Christianity*. Lewis claims to be defending the great central traditions of the Church, but the Virgin Mary is one of those central traditions. Her prominence in the literature and culture of the Middle Ages* and Renaissance undermines Lewis's credibility as a critic, as well as the principles upon which his arguments are based. A reading of Christianity that ignores any great tradition cannot be presented as a representative of it.[4]

Lewis's treatment of doctrines like the Trinity* (the Father, the Son, and the Holy Ghost), heaven and hell, and Christ's return to earth also discloses certain presuppositions. His assumptions about issues including free will, the infallibility of Scripture, and divine sovereignty (or rule) were sometimes at odds with the theologies (interpretations of scriptural truth and the nature of God) of Christians from the different Protestant denominations or those from a Roman Catholic background. And while his defense of such doctrines was primarily through rational and logical arguments, he often failed to take into account contemporary and historical theological positions. Consequently, *Mere Christianity* fails to address certain theological issues.

But while many of Lewis's arguments may no longer be valid in theological or philosophical circles, his work remains significant for contemporary debate about God and religion. His clear analogies and simple logic still provide strong arguments for belief in God and, in particular, Christian doctrine. *Mere Christianity* is still considered one of the most important defenses of Christianity ever to have been produced.[5]

NOTES

1   Walter Hooper, *C. S. Lewis: A Companion & Guide* (New York: HarperCollins, 1966), 328.

2   Scott Larsen, *Indelible Ink: 22 Prominent Christian Leaders Discuss the Books That Shape Their Faith* (Colorado Springs, CO: WaterBrook Press, 2003).

3   C. S. Lewis, *The Lion, the Witch and the Wardrobe* (New York: Collier/ Macmillan, 1970), 45.

4   See Joseph Pearce, *C. S. Lewis and the Catholic Church* (San Francisco: Ignatius, 2003), Kindle edition.

5   See Larsen, *Indelible Ink*.

MODULE 8
PLACE IN THE AUTHOR'S WORK

KEY POINTS

- The wide range of Lewis's work—from academic studies to children's fiction—helps popularize complex theological* ideas for a wide audience.

- The defense of Christianity that Lewis advanced in *Mere Christianity* appeared in, and influenced, many of his other works.

- Although Lewis is best remembered for his children's books, *Mere Christianity* remains the most widely read of his works among evangelical* Christians.

Positioning

C. S. Lewis's body of work is vast. As well as works of Christian theology, such as *Mere Christianity*, Lewis wrote children's literature, fantasy and science fiction, autobiography, poetry, and literary criticism. Much of his work has little to do with his professional career as a scholar of medieval* and Renaissance* literature at Oxford and Cambridge. He is probably best known for his children's series of Narnia fantasies, in particular *The Lion, the Witch and the Wardrobe* (1950), which is still very popular today. Yet despite the success of his novels, Lewis's academic writings remain important for students and scholars of English literature.

By the time Lewis published *Mere Christianity* in 1952 he had been a Christian for over 20 years and had already published other religious texts.

Allegorical works such as *The Pilgrim's Regress: An Allegorical Apology for Christianity, Reason and Romanticism* (1933), *The Screwtape Letters*

> **❝** God created things which had free will. That means creatures which can go either wrong or right. Some people think they can imagine a creature which was free but had no possibility of going wrong; I cannot. If a thing is free to be good it is also free to be bad. And free will is what has made evil possible. **❞**
>
> C. S. Lewis, *Mere Christianity*

(1941), and *The Great Divorce* (1944) all defended traditional Christianity. These books were all fictionalized accounts of journeys. They aimed to expose, as fallacies, common objections to Christian ideas of transcendence*—its foundation in a spiritual, rather than physical, cosmos. These texts were a way to popularize theological ideas of Christianity with a readership that would not engage with specialized theological works. Lewis always emphasized that, while he wrote on theological topics, he never considered himself a theologian. All his writings are marked by a unique style, characterized by simple and logical explanations of Christian doctrine, tied to practical illustrations.

In all these books Lewis harnesses his reason, historical knowledge, literary skill, and sense of humor to communicate often difficult truths to as wide an audience as possible. This hard-to-achieve simplicity may be why *Mere Christianity* has enjoyed immense popularity among average Christians but receives little notice from mainstream academic theologians. Whether in his fiction or prose, Lewis's work was shaped profoundly by his Christian faith. And, in some ways, *Mere Christianity* provides a simple summary and defense of those beliefs.

Integration

Amongst his lay readership, Lewis's writings have inspired many to consider arguments for the Christian faith. But some Anglican* bishops dismissed his writings as the work of an amateur theologian. As the British writer P. H. Brazier notes, "Lewis was deemed to be not qualified—he was not one of them. Some clergy within the Church of England regarded him as an outsider who had strayed into theology without being qualified to speak on the subject."[1] Nevertheless, Lewis's continued influence as an apologist,* author, and academic can be seen today. The copies of his books sold run into the millions, and his work and been translated into over 30 languages. His works remain important for their clarity, imagination, and accessibility.

It is interesting to note how Lewis has been remembered. In the United States he is primarily celebrated for his work as an apologist and for his contribution to the defense of Christianity in the modern world. This was highlighted by the centenary celebrations that took place in 1998 at the American C. S. Lewis Foundation. In Britain, however, the centenary highlighted Lewis's success as a children's author; the event was commemorated with a stamp remembering *The Lion, the Witch and the Wardrobe*. Whatever the reasons for this divergence, it is clear that Lewis's writings were so diverse and so successful that they allowed him to be remembered for different things.

Significance

For a writer with such a wide range of successful publications, it is difficult to assess which of Lewis's texts is the most important. He could be described as a man who had three careers—as a scholar, a writer of fiction, and a theologian—and succeeded in all of them. The influence of *Mere Christianity* was most significant in evangelical Christian circles, but its impact can also be seen in both the Roman Catholic* and Protestant* Churches—the two principal branches of the Christian faith. Despite his popularity among evangelical Christians, Lewis was always an Anglican (a member of the Protestant Church of England) who stuck to orthodox* tradition but never aligned himself with any particular wing of the Church.

Lewis's achievements cannot be underestimated. His academic work in English literature earned him a post at Oxford University and a prestigious professorship at Cambridge University. Yet his scholarship represents some of his least well known work, despite the contribution he made to his field of English and Renaissance* literature. Lewis's most significant popularity came through his children's and fantasy stories. Highly successful when they were written, they retain their popularity throughout the world today.

These books contributed to Lewis's establishment as a Christian author; one does not have to wander far into his fictional world of Narnia before confronting themes of God, morality, death, resurrection, and new life. And having already established himself as a Christian author with his fictional work, Lewis was able to reach a wider audience with *Mere Christianity*.

NOTES

1   P. H. Brazier, C. S. Lewis: Revelation, Conversion, and Apologetics (Eugene, OR: Pickwick, 2012), 134.

SECTION 3
IMPACT

MODULE 9
THE FIRST RESPONSES

KEY POINTS

- As an "amateur" theologian* and philosopher, Lewis's arguments were often criticized for lacking depth.

- Lewis continued to argue against naturalism*—the belief that we can only understand the world through scientific observation.

- Though Lewis's work was criticized by academic theologians and philosophers, *Mere Christianity* was received positively by the public.

Criticism

The most famous criticism of C. S. Lewis came from the English philosopher Elizabeth Anscombe.* In 1948 she argued against Lewis's ideas about naturalism as expressed in his book *Miracles*, which preceded *Mere Christianity*. In it, Lewis argues that naturalism—the belief that only physical reality exists—is self-contradictory. Anscombe claimed, however, that Lewis's arguments were based on the ambiguous use of key terms that he failed to define appropriately. For her, "all human behavior, including thought, could be accounted for by scientific causal laws."[1] In contrast, Lewis argues that humans experience insights that go beyond the natural world.

Lewis was also criticized for failing to examine the theological issues he addressed in enough depth, and for failing to take into account contemporary and historical theological positions. In 1958 the prolific American theologian Norman Pittinger* published a critique of Lewis in the leading weekly magazine *The Christian Century*. In the article, titled "Apologist versus Apologist," he accused

> **❝** I can find little ... that is good to say about Mr. Lewis as a Christian apologist and amateur theologian. It is my opinion that he has used his brilliant ... style to commend a version of Christianity which is often not even 'orthodox' ... and which in any event is frequently incredible ... He teaches a version of the Christian faith which is ... dubiously orthodox by the narrowest standards, but is also a kind of uncriticized 'traditionalism' which is stated with such eloquence and brilliance that it deceives those who are not instructed and misleads many who are. **❞**
>
> W. Norman Pittinger, "Apologist versus Apologist"

Lewis's work of being flawed. He argued that it did not consider a long tradition of academic biblical criticism, supported nonsensical readings of Christianity that ignored objective evidence against them, and overrelied on Church tradition. He also criticized Lewis's presentation of God as a hypostatized* entity—that is, a single being that is both fully human and divine.

Pittinger criticizs the unbalanced emphasis on the divine in Lewis's presentation of Christ. He argues that this downplays Christ's human characteristics—death, suffering, his presence in human time—in favor of the supernatural (the eternal and omnipresent). The American theologian Gary J. Dorrien* notes that "Pittinger despaired that many people obtained their understanding of Christianity from Lewis."[2] While Pittinger shows deep admiration for Lewis's persuasive and accessible style, it is this accessibility that makes him conclude that Lewis is "a dangerous apologist and an inept theologian."[3]

Responses

Lewis's response to his critics was to stress that the purpose of *Mere Christianity* was to provide an apologetic* for belief in the Christian

God. It was not to delve into great religious debates. Of these debates he writes, "If any topic could be relied upon to wreck a book about 'mere' Christianity—if any topic makes utterly unprofitable reading for those who do not yet believe that the Virgin's son is God—surely this is it."[4] Lewis knew that an apologetic for the orthodox* beliefs of Christianity was bound to draw criticism from the religion's various denominations.* Nonetheless he held steadfastly to his defense of what it means to call oneself a "Christian" in the simplest sense of the word.

That said, Lewis did revise his position on naturalism following his debate with Anscombe. The American philosopher Victor Reppert* notes that in the 1959 revision of *Miracles*, Lewis de-emphasized the idea that naturalism was irrational.[5] Although he remained skeptical of naturalist theories, this subtle change in language does suggest a slight shift in his views. While Lewis concedes that there is nothing irrational about natural causation, he maintains that there is nothing inherently rational about it either. He also responded to Pittinger's criticism of his hypostatic understanding of God. Lewis argued that he does emphasize the human character of Christ. He also pointed to the "humanity" of the Aslan–Christ figure in *The Chronicles of Narnia* (1950–6). As a lion, Aslan bleeds and suffers, indicating, more than his divinity, his animal or complete human nature.

Conflict and Consensus

The greatest difficulty in evaluating the merit of the criticisms leveled against Lewis lies in the nature of what Lewis was trying to achieve. He was not writing for an academic audience—or for a theologically astute audience. It is, therefore, potentially unhelpful to judge his arguments against an academic standard. Lewis admits that he is not a theologian and that he only seeks to present simple, logical arguments for the Christian faith that could be understood by the average person. This does not mean that Lewis's ideas should remain unchallenged in certain areas, but it does mean that certain criticisms should be seen in the light of what the book was trying to achieve. *Mere Christianity* was not meant to be a theological or philosophical treatise, nor was it a presentation of Lewis's personal religion. Instead, it is an apologetic for the basic principles and doctrines of the Christian faith.[6]

Despite theological and philosophical criticisms, Lewis did not revise *Mere Christianity*. Instead he continued to defend his rationalistic* position that we can reach the truth through the exercise of reason. With regard to the debate about naturalism, Lewis maintains the idea that human beings reach true conclusions through reason. He also maintains that reason is best understood through theistic metaphysics* instead of naturalistic metaphysics*—that is, through the belief that God exists beyond natural experience, and not by denying the supernatural. No consensus was reached between Lewis and his naturalist opponents and the debate continues today.

NOTES

1   Elizabeth Anscombe, quoted in John Owens, "C. S. Lewis's Argument against Naturalism," in *A Myth Retold: Re-Encountering C. S. Lewis as Theologian*, ed. Martin Sutherland (Eugene, OR: Wipf and Stock, 2014), 58.

2   Gary J. Dorrien, *The Making of American Liberal Theology: Crisis, Irony, and Postmodernity 1950–2005* (Louisville, KY: John Knox Press, 2005), 195.

3   W. Norman Pittinger, "Apologist versus Apologist: A Critique of C. S. Lewis as 'Defender of the Faith,'" *Christian Century* LXXV (1958): 1107.

4   C. S. Lewis, *Mere Christianity*, 50th edn (London: HarperCollins, 2001), VIII.

5   See Victor Reppert, *C. S. Lewis's Dangerous Idea: In Defense of the Argument of Reason* (Downers Grove, IL: InterVarsity Press, 2003).

6   For more perspectives on Lewis, see M. Ward and R. MacSwain, eds, *The Cambridge Companion to C. S. Lewis* (Cambridge: Cambridge University Press, 2010).

MODULE 10
THE EVOLVING DEBATE

KEY POINTS

- Lewis's text remains relevant today because it deals with two issues that continue to matter: the logic of belief and the personal experience of belief.

- *Mere Christianity* continues to be widely used both as a defense of religion and as a guide to what it means to be a Christian.

- Contemporary philosophers have adapted and developed some of Lewis's arguments against naturalism.*

Uses and Problems

Since C. S. Lewis published *Mere Christianity*, the West has undergone a significant cultural shift, even if Lewis's ideas are still used in the field of apologetics* and among mainstream Christian Churches.

In very general terms, there has been a movement away from the modernist* idea that reality can be explained by scientific or objective truths. According to postmodernist* thought, there is no absolute truth—an idea that has affected both academic and social spheres. While modernism leans toward rational, objective thought, postmodernism emphasizes experiential, subjective knowledge over abstract principles. What is unique about Lewis is that, in some ways, he acts as a bridge between modernism and postmodernism. He makes rational arguments for objective truth, while emphasizing experiential knowledge. Lewis's concern for both logic and experience in *Mere Christianity* means that his text continues to be relevant in contemporary debates.

> **"** Everyone has warned me not to tell you what I am going to tell you in this last book. They all say 'the ordinary reader does not want Theology; give him plain practical religion'. I have rejected their advice. **"**

C. S. Lewis, *Mere Christianity*

Mere Christianity has proven to be one of the most groundbreaking defenses of the Christian faith in the modern world. While it is not a seminal text in the academic fields of theology* or philosophy, it stands as one of the most successful and lucid accounts of the elementary doctrines of the Christian faith. Perhaps it was because Lewis approached theology as an "outsider," and expanded the genre of theology to include his fantasy literature, that he has emerged as a prominent figure in Christian apologetics for the modern era. Whatever the reason, his use of evocative illustrations, literary conventions, and philosophical reasoning has made him a major voice of the twentieth century.

Schools of Thought

Mere Christianity is not a starting point for new ideas. It takes people back to the basics and offers a compelling, simple account of what it means to be a Christian. As a result, while Lewis's writing has not produced a particular school of thought, it has inspired many of his readers to consider arguments for the Christian faith. And while some scholars in the fields of philosophy or theology often dismiss his arguments as unworthy of discussion, Lewis's influence as an apologist, author, and academic can still be seen today.

Among Protestant* Christians, the famous British preacher and apologist John Stott* called *Mere Christianity* the first "good Christian book." He recommended it to all his readers in his own book *Basic Christianity* (1958).[1] Another well-known figure influenced by Lewis is the British-born Canadian theologian J. I. Packer,* who attributes

Lewis's popularity to the fact that he was a forthright speaker about mainstream Christianity and spoke in the public forum. Packer contends that despite Lewis's smoking, drinking, and somewhat unorthodox views on justification, salvation, and purgatory (the place, some Christians believe, where souls spend time between death and admittance to heaven), he remains a "Christian for all Christians."[2]

Lewis's writings and ideas have not been significantly adapted or modernized to suit contemporary audiences. Written just over half a century ago, his work continues to inspire Christians to defend Christianity through honest debate and dialogue in the public forum.

In Current Scholarship

Although *Mere Christianity* is not central to the contemporary scholarly debate in theology or philosophy, scholars such as the American philosopher of religion Alvin Pantinga* have followed up the criticisms that Lewis made about naturalism.

One particular point that Lewis raises is that while naturalists tend to deny concepts such as good and evil, they employ these concepts in their own arguments nevertheless: "A moment after they [naturalists] have admitted that good and evil are illusions, you will find them exhorting us to work for posterity, to educate, to revolutionize, liquidate, live and die for the good of the human race ... They write with indignation like men proclaiming what is good in itself and denouncing what is evil in itself, and not at all like men recording that they personally like mild beer but some prefer bitter."[3]

Some of today's naturalists, among them the British philosopher Michael Ruse* and the American biologist E. O. Wilson,* have responded to these critiques. Their response has been to denounce morality and ethics as nothing more than illusions passed on to us by our genetic makeup. Others avoid this type of strict naturalism, preferring to argue that human values and ethics simply emerged over the course of human history.

Lewis himself knew the pull of naturalism. He writes, "We all have Naturalism in our bones and even conversion does not at once work the infection out of our system. Its assumptions rush back upon the mind the moment vigilance is relaxed."[4] In his arguments against the naturalists he developed an expanded model that affirmed the existence of physical laws, but also invited people to think beyond the physical. He did not believe that being a Christian meant giving up one's love for the natural world, or one's intellectual or imaginative capacities. Instead, he saw Christianity as the fulfillment of those capacities.

NOTES

1   John R. W. Stott, *Basic Christianity* (London: InterVarsity Press, 1958).

2   Justin Phillips, *C. S. Lewis at the BBC* (London: HarperCollins, 2002), 287–8.

3   C. S. Lewis, *Miracles: A Preliminary Study* (New York: Macmillan, 1960), 40–1.

4   Lewis, *Miracles*, 168.

IMPACT AND INFLUENCE TODAY

KEY POINTS

- Some of the arguments Lewis used have been rendered out of date by scientific discoveries.

- Some of Lewis's positions, such as his notion of "just war," continue to have an influence on modern ethical debates.

- Although it has had limited impact in academic circles, *Mere Christianity* continues to influence lay people exploring the Christian faith.

Position

Although C. S. Lewis's *Mere Christianity* still influences the field of Christian apologetics,* scientific developments since its publication have meant that some of his ideas have had to evolve.

One of the great advances since Lewis's time has been the work undertaken in contemporary physics. It is now generally accepted that randomness exists at the quantum-mechanical* level—that is, on the smallest measurable scales. For Lewis, the indeterminate nature of the world was one of the flaws in naturalism. He argues that naturalism* is deterministic*—that is, if life is determined by material causes, it must unfold in a set way. If this were true, the indeterminate nature of the universe, as revealed by modern physics, would lead to a breakdown of the naturalist position.

But most naturalists today accept quantum mechanics. They do not believe that quantum randomness contradicts the idea that all events happen as a result of natural processes. In fact, both Lewis's contemporary and his current critics have suggested that he did not understand the core of the naturalist argument. They argue that it was

> ❝ That is why the Christian is in a different position from other people who are trying to be good. They hope, by being good, to please God if there is one; or—if they think there is not—at least they hope to deserve approval from good men. But the Christian thinks any good he does comes from the Christ-life inside him. He does not think God will love us because we are good, but that God will make us good because He loves us; just as the roof of a greenhouse does not attract the sun because it is bright, but becomes bright because the sun shines on it. ❞
>
> C. S. Lewis, *Mere Christianity*

this that led him (mistakenly) to view naturalism as deterministic.

Contemporary naturalists, such as the British biologist and author Richard Dawkins,* continue to argue against Lewis's position. In texts such as *The God Delusion* (2006), Dawkins argues that evolution* reveals a world without design and that the physical order of the universe is causally closed. In which case nothing transcendent*—the Christian God, for example—has any effect on the natural world. Other naturalists such as the American biologist Ursula Goodenough* and the American anthropologist Terrence Deacon* have tried to explain reason through the term "emergence." This concept alludes to the way in which new qualities can appear in the natural world through a multiplicity of simple interactions.[1]

It is questionable, however, whether the physical micro-processes of the natural world can account for the human ability to think or reason. Instead, some will argue that human reasoning is a purposeful activity that moves beyond our simple physical attributes. To have rational thoughts or beliefs requires more than the motion of atoms inside the brain.

Interaction

One issue raised in *Mere Christianity* still discussed today is whether it is ethical for a Christian to participate in war.

Lewis was familiar with the "just war" theories of the early Christian theologian Saint Augustine,* the Italian Dominican friar Thomas Aquinas,* and the sixteenth-century English theologian Richard Hooker.* He also had firsthand experience of war himself. While he was not a pacifist, Lewis was very ambivalent about war and the horrors it produces. For Lewis, war seems to have been a matter of duty to defend one's country. If a Christian were called to serve, they should do so virtuously and without regret. He writes, "War is a dreadful thing, and I can respect an honest pacifist, though I think he is entirely mistaken."[2] He went on to argue that killing in war and committing murder are different in the biblical understanding and that the former can be morally acceptable. Lewis does not glorify war or killing but sees it as part of an imperfect world.

The contemporary American theologian Stanley Hauerwas* argues that these arguments are not convincing; Lewis, he says, fails to address the practices of Christian pacifism. While Hauerwas agrees that killing is not an absolute evil, he argues that human beings were not created to kill and that the overall life of Christ provides a model for non-violence. Hauerwas concludes by arguing that sustained non-violence is the calling of the Christian community despite the realities of war. To illustrate truly Christian behavior he points to the lion Aslan's martyrdom in Lewis's *The Lion, the Witch and the Wardrobe*. In the book, Aslan offers himself as a sacrifice to save the life of a child, Edmund. Hauerwas says this exemplifies the highest form of selfless love and sacrifice against the violence of the world.[3]

The Continuing Debate

While Lewis is not considered influential in current theological or philosophical circles, there are those who have been profoundly affected by *Mere Christianity*. Notable examples include Thomas Monaghan, the American founder of Domino's Pizza, a pizza-delivery/takeout restaurant with branches across the globe. After reading *Mere Christianity*—especially the chapter on "pride"—Monaghan divested his fortune, sold his private helicopter and expensive cars, and gave over £600 million to charity.[4] Although not all stories of life-change are as dramatic, the force and simplicity of Lewis's arguments have the potential to reshape people's lives.

There are scientists, too, who have been affected by Lewis's rational arguments for God. The American geneticist Francis Collins,* for example, is the leader of the Human Genome Project,* an international research project that aims to map the human genome. He currently serves as the director of the National Institutes of Health in America. In graduate school, Collins was a proclaimed atheist.* But he began to question his religious beliefs when he regularly found himself surrounded by dying patients at the hospital.[5] He read *Mere Christianity* and was convinced by Lewis's arguments. He later became a Christian and went on to write *The Language of God: A Scientist Presents Evidence for Belief* (2006), which became a *New York Times* bestseller.

NOTES

1   See Ursula Goodenough and Terrence W. Deacon, "The Sacred Emergence of Nature," in *The Oxford Handbook of Religion and Science*, ed. Philip Clayton and Zachary Simpson (Oxford: Oxford University Press, 2008), 853–71.

2   C. S. Lewis, *Mere Christianity*, 50th edn (London: HarperCollins, 2001), 119.

3   Stanley Hauerwas, "On Violence," in *The Cambridge Companion to C. S. Lewis*, ed. Robert MacSwain and Michael Ward (Cambridge: Cambridge University Press, 2010), 189–202.

4   See Bruce L. Edwards, *C. S. Lewis: Apologist, Philosopher, and Theologian* (Westport, CT: Praeger, 2007), 52.

5   Francis S. Collins, *The Language of God: A Scientist Presents Evidence for Belief* (New York: Simon & Schuster, 2006), 21.

MODULE 12
WHERE NEXT?

KEY POINTS

- Lewis's clarity and his ability to present arguments in a simple yet convincing manner mean that *Mere Christianity* remains an important text.

- The adaptation and expansion of Lewis's ideas by other writers continues to draw readers to back to the text.

- *Mere Christianity* continues to influence cultures around the world. It is one of the great apologetic* works of the twentieth century.

Potential

There is little doubt that C. S. Lewis's *Mere Christianity* will continue to be influential as an apologetic for Christianity. Its clarity and style make it accessible to a wide audience. Most people who read the book will appreciate Lewis's skill in connecting ideas and the simplicity with which he presents logical arguments. They will also appreciate his use of metaphor, imagination, humor, and myth as ways of understanding the Christian faith.

Another reason that *Mere Christianity* will continue to be influential is because the variety of Lewis's writing has won him such a range of readers. Lewis wrote nearly 40 books during his lifetime, with collections of essays, letters, sermons, and stories published after his death. As a result, many readers find *Mere Christianity* while exploring Lewis's other writings. Some have discovered Lewis through their encounters with *The Chronicles of Narnia* (1950), whether through the book series or the popular film productions. Many of the arguments developed in *Mere Christianity* are also expressed in these children's

> **❝** The point is not that God will refuse you admission to His eternal world if you have not got certain qualities of character: the point is that if people have not got at least the beginnings of those qualities inside them, then no possible external conditions could make a 'Heaven' for them—that is, could make them happy with the deep, strong, unshakable kind of happiness God intends for us. **❞**
>
> C. S. Lewis, *Mere Christianity*

stories. Others might come across Lewis by way of the biographical film *Shadowlands*, a dramatization of Lewis's life and marriage to the writer Joy Davidman.[*][1] Some might read Lewis's science fiction, or other apologetic works, or read his scholarly writing on English literature. Lewis's popularity on so many different levels is likely to mean that *Mere Christianity* will continue to be discovered and read by future generations.

Future Directions

Lewis's core ideas in *Mere Christianity* continue to be developed by those who have studied his religious thinking. These include the American author Will Vaus,[*] whose book *Mere Theology* (2004) offers a systematic treatment of Lewis's theology.[*] The American academic David C. Downing[*] examines Lewis's mysticism in his writings in *Into the Region of Awe* (2005), while *Pleasures Forevermore: The Theology of C. S. Lewis* (1983), by the American author John Randolph Willis,[*] explores the theological principles that underlie Lewis's apologetics and fiction from a Roman Catholic[*] perspective.[2]

Some works focus on Lewis's theological arguments: the American academic Peter Kreeft's[*] book *C. S. Lewis for the Third Millennium: Six Essays on The Abolition of Man* (1994) defends Lewis's idea of natural law and applies it to the challenges of contemporary culture. Still others approach Lewis from a devotional perspective, and works like *C. S. Lewis: Spirituality for Mere Christians* (1998), by the American writer William Griffin,* offer insights into spiritual practice and devotion.[3]

Whether atheist* or merely undecided, Protestant* or Roman Catholic, *Mere Christianity* has had an impact on people from a variety of backgrounds and religious beliefs. At a time when doctrinal* divisions between Christian denominations* continue to run high, Lewis's work lays the groundwork for dialogue. It speaks to both Christians and non-Christians about the fundamentals of faith. Lewis never intended *Mere Christianity* to be a work that would attract future disciples. His hope was to convince others of the truth of the Christian faith.

Summary

Lewis's breadth of knowledge, his vivid imagination, and his ability to communicate complex ideas in simple language found expression in a particularly distinctive work. His contribution was considerable: in *Mere Christianity* Lewis demonstrated that it is possible for an educated layperson to speak with the same authority as a priest or theologian on theological matters. In fact, he demonstrated that it was possible for a layperson to be more effective in communicating theological truths than someone who was ordained. His style is clear and straightforward. It brings to life aspects of Christian doctrine that make the moral and ethical beliefs of Christianity applicable to contemporary culture. There is a timelessness and lucidity to his ideas that make his work as important today as it was during his own time.

As an apologetic work, *Mere Christianity* continues to have an impact in cultures around the world.[4] Even though Lewis held firmly to the idea of absolute truth—which contrasts with the postmodern* claim that there are no absolutes—his honest, non-partisan approach to Christianity is a breath of fresh air. He did not claim any authority on theological matters; instead, he offered up his arguments for public debate so that their truth might be tested by anyone.

Lewis's reputation will always be connected to his popularity as a children's author, but *Mere Christianity* is his most successful apologetic as an "amateur" theologian. In nearly all of his works we find an underlying theme: the discussion of every person's journey towards God. Some are closer, some are further away, but all are encouraged to move in the direction of God. In the final Chronicle of Narnia, *The Last Battle*, the repeated refrain "further up and further in" sums up Lewis's understanding of the faith journey—it is a never ending process. But all people are urged to move along the path towards God.

NOTES

1   C. S. Lewis, *Surprised by Joy: The Shape of My Early Life* (New York: Harcourt Brace, 1955).

2   See Will Vaus, *Mere Theology: A Guide to the Thought of C. S. Lewis* (Downers Grove, IL: InterVarsity, 2004); David C. Downing, *Into the Region of Awe: Mysticism in C. S. Lewis* (Downers Grove, IL: InterVarsity, 2005); John Randolph Willis, *Pleasures Forevermore: The Theology of C. S. Lewis* (Chicago: Loyola, 1983).

3   See Peter Kreeft, *C. S. Lewis for the Third Millennium: Six Essays on The Abolition of Man* (San Francisco: Ignatius Press, 1994); William Griffin, *C. S. Lewis: Spirituality for Mere Christians* (New York: Crossroad, 1998).

4   Mark Noll, "C. S. Lewis's 'Mere Christianity' (the Book and the Ideal) at the Start of the Twenty-first Century," *VII: An Anglo-American Literary Review* 19 (2002): 31–44.

GLOSSARY

GLOSSARY OF TERMS

Anglican: a member of the Church of England, the official state Church in England.

Apologetics: the defensive method of argument for justifying a religious faith.

Atheism: the position or belief that a God or gods do not exist.

British Broadcasting Corporation (BBC): a public corporation mainly financed by a television license fee set by the British government, which provides much of the television and radio broadcasting for the country.

Darwinism: theories associated with the British naturalist Charles Darwin, who was famous for setting out the theory of evolution by natural selection.

Demythologize: to remove mythic elements from a story, legend, and so on. In theology this means to strip the miraculous from the text in order to analyze it purely from a historical perspective.

Denomination: different factions of Christianity. After the Protestant Reformation, Christianity divided into smaller groups, determined by their particular faith and practice.

Determinism: a philosophical theory proposing that all experiences are determined by causes regarded as external to the will. This includes moral choices, which some philosophers have taken to mean that human beings have no free will and, therefore, cannot be held responsible for their actions.

Doctrine: a set of beliefs, often those of a religion or a political party.

Enlightenment: an intellectual movement that began in Europe in the seventeenth and eighteenth centuries. It emphasized the use of reason and scientific knowledge and challenged traditional religious faith.

Evangelicalism: a form of Christian faith that emphasizes personal conversion and actively expressing the biblical message of Christ to others.

Evangelize: to preach or proclaim the Gospel.

Evolution: a scientific theory developed by Charles Darwin that is the keystone of modern biology. It proposes that animals and other living populations have their origin in other preexisting types that have changed over successive generations.

Human Genome Project: an international research project in the sciences that investigates the sequencing of all the genetic content of human organisms.

Hypostasis: in theology, this refers to the shared existence of a human and a divine nature. In philosophy it refers to a being's underlying substance, in contrast to its attributes.

Inklings: a literary discussion group comprising J. R. R. Tolkien, Owen Barfield, Nevill Coghill, Lord David Cecil, Charles Williams, and C. S. Lewis's brother Warren.

Jesuit: a member of the Society of Jesus, an esteemed Roman Catholic order founded by St. Ignatius of Loyola.

Materialism: a philosophical view stating that all facts about humanity are causally dependent on physical processes.

Methodism: a Christian denomination. Formerly united with the Anglican Church, the Methodist movement led by John Wesley broke away and established a new denomination.

Middle Ages: the medieval period in European history between the fall of the Roman Empire in 476 C.E. and the emergence of the Renaissance in the fourteenth century. It is characterized by a feudal system of government where land ownership defined power relations.

Modernism: a twentieth-century movement that, in theology, moved away from traditional beliefs and doctrines of the Church in accordance with the findings of modern criticism and research.

Naturalism: in philosophy, this is the belief that we can only come to know the world through scientific observation and testing, rather than through spiritual guidance.

Naturalistic metaphysics: the belief that nothing exists beyond the natural world.

Orthodox: of, belonging to, or in accordance with the accepted theological or ecclesiastical doctrines of a particular religion; practices or beliefs conforming with these doctrines.

Pantheism: in philosophy, this is the theory that the universe and God are identical. God, therefore, is everything and, conversely, everything is God.

Postmodernism: a broad term referring to a philosophical outlook that takes a skeptical, and often ironic, approach to truth claims.

Premodern: a period before the age of science and reason (roughly the seventeenth to the eighteenth centuries) where an emphasis was placed on religious faith and tradition as a source of truth.

Presbyterianism: a Protestant denomination that was formed around particular doctrinal beliefs and a "Presbyterian" form of governance led by a group of elders.

Protestantism: a branch of the Christian faith founded in the sixteenth century following the schism with the Roman Catholic Church known as "the Reformation." Protestantism differs from Roman Catholicism on certain understandings of the significance of ritual and on Church hierarchy, among other things.

Quantum mechanics: the mathematical description of the motion and interaction of atomic and subatomic particles that was developed from the old quantum theory and incorporates the concept of wave–particle duality, the uncertainty principle, and the correspondence principle; the branch of physics concerned with this.

Rationalism: the argument that rational thought is all that is required to reach true conclusions; faith and Scripture, for example, are not required.

Renaissance: a period of cultural history following the Middle Ages in which European arts, architecture, music, and literature were reinvigorated by a turn towards classical—ancient Greek and Roman—models.

Roman Catholicism: the Christian Church established in Rome under the authority of the Pope. This is the largest Christian Church worldwide and is governed by bishops who work under the sole authority of the Pope.

Secular: describes what belongs to the world and its affairs as distinguished from the Church or other religions.

Secularism: a social theory that moves away from belief in God or otherworldliness toward human life on earth.

Theism: the belief in one god, as opposed to polytheism (the belief in multiple gods) or pantheism (the belief that God and the universe are one).

Theistic metaphysics: the belief that God's existence is greater and outside of natural experience.

Theology: the systematic study of the nature of God, usually conducted with recourse to Scripture.

Transcendent: surpassing the range of normal or physical human experience.

Trinity: the Christian belief that God exists in the three persons of the Father, Son, and Holy Spirit.

World War I: an international conflict from 1914 to 1918 centered in Europe and involving the major economic world powers of the day. The industrial advancements in military technology as well as the scale of the conflict resulted in vast military and civilian casualties.

World War II: global conflict from 1939 to 1945 that involved the world's great powers and numerous other countries around the globe. Fought between the Allies (the United States, Britain, France, the Soviet Union, and others) and the Axis powers (Germany, Italy, Japan, and others), it was seen as a major moral struggle between freedom and tyranny and included events like the Holocaust.

PEOPLE MENTIONED IN THE TEXT

Elizabeth Anscombe (1919–2001) was a philosopher at Oxford University and later became professor of philosophy at Cambridge University. She publically debated with Lewis at the Oxford Socratic Club on February 2, 1948.

Thomas Aquinas (1225–74) was a medieval monk who had a major influence on the Church through his theological and philosophical writings. His most influential work was *Summa Theologica* (1265–74).

Aristotle (384–322 B.C.E.) was a Greek philosopher and scientist. He was one of the most influential thinkers in Western society in metaphysics, politics, and the sciences.

Augustine of Hippo (354–430 C.E.) was a Christian theologian and bishop whose writings had a significant impact on the Church. His most famous works are *Confessions* (398 C.E.) and *The City of God* (426 C.E.).

Owen Barfield (1898–1997) was a British solicitor. He was widely published as a non-academic in the fields of English language, literature, and philosophy.

Richard Baxter (1615–91) was an English Puritan Church leader. His work and writings were influential among the nonconformist Christians of the Protestant Reformation.

Rudolf Bultmann (1884–1976) was a German theologian and one of the major figures in liberal biblical studies in the twentieth century.

John Calvin (1509–64) was a French theologian and Protestant Reformer. His *Institutes of Christian Religion* is considered one of the great systematic doctrines of Reformed Christianity.

Gilbert Keith Chesterton (1874–1936) was an English author, theologian, and philosopher. He is well known for his detective-priest Father Brown short stories and for defending the idea of the common man.

Francis Collins (b. 1950) is an American physicist and geneticist. He is known for directing the Human Genome Project.

Charles Darwin (1809–82) was an English naturalist, celebrated for describing the processes by which biological evolution occurs. He first put forward his theory of "natural selection" in his groundbreaking book *On the Origin of Species* (1859).

Joy Davidman (1915–60) was an American writer who married C. S. Lewis in 1956. She died from cancer four years later.

Richard Dawkins (b. 1941) is an English evolutionary biologist who held the position of professor for public understanding of science at Oxford from 1995 until 2008. He is well known for his criticism of religion.

Terrence Deacon is a professor of anthropology at the University of California, Berkeley.

Ursula Goodenough (b. 1943) is professor of biology at Washington University, and is noted for the book *Sacred Depths of Nature* (1998).

Stanley Hauerwas (b. 1940) is an American theologian and ethicist who teaches at Duke University, North Carolina. His major works include *The Peaceable Kingdom* (1991) which is a substantial introduction to Christian ethics.

Richard Hooker (1554–1600) was an Anglican priest and theologian. He was influential in the formation of the Church of England after it separated from the Roman Catholic Church.

George MacDonald (1824–1905) was a little-known Scottish minister who wrote several fantasy books that were made popular by Lewis. The most influential of MacDonald's books on Lewis was *Phantastes* (1858).

Peter Milward (b. 1925) is a Jesuit priest and literary scholar. He is professor emeritus at Sophia University in Tokyo, Japan.

J. I. Packer (b. 1926) is a British-born Canadian Christian theologian who taught at Regent College in Vancouver, B.C. He is considered one of the most influential evangelical Christians in North America.

Alvin Pantinga (b. 1932) is an American philosopher most noted for his apologetics of the Christian faith. He taught at the University of Notre Dame and has written *Warranted Christian Belief* (2000).

William Norman Pittinger (1905–97) was an American Anglican priest and prolific theologian. He is known for his interest in process theology, which regards God not as an eternal and unchanging figure, but as a presence closely involved and influenced by temporal processes.

Plato (c. 429–347 B.C.E.) was a Greek philosopher and disciple of Socrates. He founded the Academy in Athens and is one of the most influential philosophers of Western history.

Michael Ruse (b. 1940) is a philosopher of science with a specialty in dealing with the relationship between science and religion. Ruse's popular book *Darwinism and Its Discontents* (2006) argues for a Christian understanding of evolution compatible with biblical teachings.

John Stott (1921–2011) was a leading evangelical Anglican and vicar of All Souls Church, Langham Place (London). He wrote extensively and established the Langham Partnership International, which promoted Christian teaching worldwide.

J. R. R. Tolkien (1892–1973) was a writer and professor at Oxford University who specialized in Anglo-Saxon literature and philology. He is renowned for his series of fantasy books *The Lord of the Rings* (1954–5) and *The Hobbit* (1937)

Virgin Mary: the mother of Jesus Christ who is believed to have been impregnated by the Spirit of God and never engaged in sexual relations.

E. O. Wilson (b. 1929) is an American biologist known for his work in biodiversity and environmental advocacy. He has twice won the Pulitzer Prize for General Non-Fiction and has written bestsellers such as *Letters to a Young Scientist* (2013) and *The Meaning of Human Existence* (2014).

WORKS CITED

WORKS CITED

Baxter, Richard. *The Practical Works of Richard Baxter*. London: Paternoster Row, 1838.

Brazier, P. H. *C. S. Lewis: Revelation, Conversion, and Apologetics*. Eugene, OR: Pickwick, 2012.

Collins, Francis S. *The Language of God: A Scientist Presents Evidence for Belief*. New York: Simon & Schuster, 2006.

Dockery, David S. "Books of the Century." *Christianity Today*, April 24, 2000. Accessed September 8, 2015. http://www.christianitytoday.com/ct/2000/april24/5.92.html.

Dorrien, Gary J. *The Making of American Liberal Theology: Crisis, Irony, and Postmodernity 1950–2005*. Louisville, KY: John Knox Press, 2005.

Downing, David C. *Into the Region of Awe: Mysticism in C. S. Lewis*. Downers Grove, IL: InterVarsity, 2005.

Duriez, Colin. *The A–Z of C. S. Lewis: An Encyclopaedia of His Life, Thought, and Writings*. Oxford: Lion Hudson, 2013.

Edwards, Bruce L. *C. S. Lewis: Apologist, Philosopher, and Theologian*. Westport, CT: Praeger, 2007.

Goodenough, Ursula, and Terrence W. Deacon. "The Sacred Emergence of Nature." In *The Oxford Handbook of Religion and Science*, edited by Philip Clayton and Zachary Simpson, 853–71. Oxford: Oxford University Press, 2008.

Griffin, William. *C. S. Lewis: Spirituality for Mere Christians*. New York: Crossroad, 1998.

Hauerwas, Stanley. "On Violence." In *The Cambridge Companion to C. S. Lewis*, edited by Robert MacSwain and Michael Ward, 189–202. Cambridge: Cambridge University Press, 2010.

Hooper, Walter. *C. S. Lewis: A Companion & Guide*. New York: HarperCollins, 1966.

Kreeft, Peter. *C. S. Lewis for the Third Millennium: Six Essays on The Abolition of Man*. San Francisco: Ignatius Press, 1994.

Larsen, Scott. *Indelible Ink: 22 Prominent Christian Leaders Discuss the Books That Shape Their Faith*. Colorado Springs, CO: WaterBrook Press, 2003.

Lewis, C. S. *The Lion, the Witch and the Wardrobe*. London: Geoffrey Bles, 1950.

Surprised by Joy: The Shape of My Early Life. New York: Harcourt Brace, 1955.

Miracles: A Preliminary Study. New York: Macmillan, 1960.

Letters to Malcomb: Chiefly on Prayer. San Diego: Harcourt Brace, 1964.

"Christian Apologetics." In *God in the Dock*, 89–103. Grand Rapids, MI: Eerdmans, 1970.

Mere Christianity. 50th edn. London: HarperCollins, 2001.

MacSwain, R., and M. Ward, eds. *The Cambridge Companion to C. S. Lewis*. Cambridge: Cambridge University Press, 2010.

Noll, Mark. "C. S. Lewis's 'Mere Christianity' (the Book and the Ideal) at the Start of the Twenty-first Century." *VII: An Anglo-American Literary Review* 19 (2002): 31–44.

Owens, John. "C. S. Lewis's Argument against Naturalism." In *A Myth Retold: Re-Encountering C. S. Lewis as Theologian*, edited by Martin Sutherland, 57–68. Eugene, OR: Wipf and Stock, 2014.

Pearce, Joseph. *C. S. Lewis and the Catholic Church*. San Francisco: Ignatius, 2003.

Phillips, Justin. *C. S. Lewis at the BBC*. London: HarperCollins, 2002.

Pittinger, W. Norman. "Apologist versus Apologist: A Critique of C. S. Lewis as 'Defender of the Faith.'" *Christian Century* LXXV (1958): 1104–7.

Purtill, Richard L. *C. S. Lewis' Case for the Christian Faith.* San Francisco: Ignatius, 2004.

Reppert, Victor. *C. S. Lewis's Dangerous Idea: In Defense of the Argument from Reason*. Downers Grove, IL: InterVarsity Press, 2003.

Stott, John R. W. *Basic Christianity.* London: InterVarsity Press, 1958.

Vaus, Will. *Mere Theology: A Guide to the Thought of C. S. Lewis*. Downers Grove, IL: InterVarsity, 2004.

Ward, W., and R. MacSwain, eds. *The Cambridge Companion to C. S. Lewis*. Cambridge: Cambridge University Press, 2010.

Willis, John Randolph. *Pleasures Forevermore: The Theology of C. S. Lewis*. Chicago: Loyola, 1983.

THE MACAT LIBRARY
BY DISCIPLINE

The Macat Library By Discipline

AFRICANA STUDIES

Chinua Achebe's *An Image of Africa: Racism in Conrad's Heart of Darkness*
W. E. B. Du Bois's *The Souls of Black Folk*
Zora Neale Huston's *Characteristics of Negro Expression*
Martin Luther King Jr's *Why We Can't Wait*
Toni Morrison's *Playing in the Dark: Whiteness in the American Literary Imagination*

ANTHROPOLOGY

Arjun Appadurai's *Modernity at Large: Cultural Dimensions of Globalisation*
Philippe Ariès's *Centuries of Childhood*
Franz Boas's *Race, Language and Culture*
Kim Chan & Renée Mauborgne's *Blue Ocean Strategy*
Jared Diamond's *Guns, Germs & Steel: the Fate of Human Societies*
Jared Diamond's *Collapse: How Societies Choose to Fail or Survive*
E. E. Evans-Pritchard's *Witchcraft, Oracles and Magic Among the Azande*
James Ferguson's *The Anti-Politics Machine*
Clifford Geertz's *The Interpretation of Cultures*
David Graeber's *Debt: the First 5000 Years*
Karen Ho's *Liquidated: An Ethnography of Wall Street*
Geert Hofstede's *Culture's Consequences: Comparing Values, Behaviors, Institutes and Organizations across Nations*
Claude Lévi-Strauss's *Structural Anthropology*
Jay Macleod's *Ain't No Makin' It: Aspirations and Attainment in a Low-Income Neighborhood*
Saba Mahmood's *The Politics of Piety: The Islamic Revival and the Feminist Subjec*t
Marcel Mauss's *The Gift*

BUSINESS

Jean Lave & Etienne Wenger's *Situated Learning*
Theodore Levitt's *Marketing Myopia*
Burton G. Malkiel's *A Random Walk Down Wall Street*
Douglas McGregor's *The Human Side of Enterprise*
Michael Porter's *Competitive Strategy: Creating and Sustaining Superior Performance*
John Kotter's *Leading Change*
C. K. Prahalad & Gary Hamel's *The Core Competence of the Corporation*

CRIMINOLOGY

Michelle Alexander's *The New Jim Crow: Mass Incarceration in the Age of Colorblindness*
Michael R. Gottfredson & Travis Hirschi's *A General Theory of Crime*
Richard Herrnstein & Charles A. Murray's *The Bell Curve: Intelligence and Class Structure in American Life*
Elizabeth Loftus's *Eyewitness Testimony*
Jay Macleod's *Ain't No Makin' It: Aspirations and Attainment in a Low-Income Neighborhood*
Philip Zimbardo's *The Lucifer Effect*

ECONOMICS

Janet Abu-Lughod's *Before European Hegemony*
Ha-Joon Chang's *Kicking Away the Ladder*
David Brion Davis's *The Problem of Slavery in the Age of Revolution*
Milton Friedman's *The Role of Monetary Policy*
Milton Friedman's *Capitalism and Freedom*
David Graeber's *Debt: the First 5000 Years*
Friedrich Hayek's *The Road to Serfdom*
Karen Ho's *Liquidated: An Ethnography of Wall Street*

John Maynard Keynes's *The General Theory of Employment, Interest and Money*
Charles P. Kindleberger's *Manias, Panics and Crashes*
Robert Lucas's *Why Doesn't Capital Flow from Rich to Poor Countries?*
Burton G. Malkiel's *A Random Walk Down Wall Street*
Thomas Robert Malthus's *An Essay on the Principle of Population*
Karl Marx's *Capital*
Thomas Piketty's *Capital in the Twenty-First Century*
Amartya Sen's *Development as Freedom*
Adam Smith's *The Wealth of Nations*
Nassim Nicholas Taleb's *The Black Swan: The Impact of the Highly Improbable*
Amos Tversky's & Daniel Kahneman's *Judgment under Uncertainty: Heuristics and Biases*
Mahbub Ul Haq's *Reflections on Human Development*
Max Weber's *The Protestant Ethic and the Spirit of Capitalism*

FEMINISM AND GENDER STUDIES

Judith Butler's *Gender Trouble*
Simone De Beauvoir's *The Second Sex*
Michel Foucault's *History of Sexuality*
Betty Friedan's *The Feminine Mystique*
Saba Mahmood's *The Politics of Piety: The Islamic Revival and the Feminist Subject*
Joan Wallach Scott's *Gender and the Politics of History*
Mary Wollstonecraft's *A Vindication of the Rights of Woman*
Virginia Woolf's *A Room of One's Own*

GEOGRAPHY

The Brundtland Report's *Our Common Future*
Rachel Carson's *Silent Spring*
Charles Darwin's *On the Origin of Species*
James Ferguson's *The Anti-Politics Machine*
Jane Jacobs's *The Death and Life of Great American Cities*
James Lovelock's *Gaia: A New Look at Life on Earth*
Amartya Sen's *Development as Freedom*
Mathis Wackernagel & William Rees's *Our Ecological Footprint*

HISTORY

Janet Abu-Lughod's *Before European Hegemony*
Benedict Anderson's *Imagined Communities*
Bernard Bailyn's *The Ideological Origins of the American Revolution*
Hanna Batatu's *The Old Social Classes And The Revolutionary Movements Of Iraq*
Christopher Browning's *Ordinary Men: Reserve Police Batallion 101 and the Final Solution in Poland*
Edmund Burke's *Reflections on the Revolution in France*
William Cronon's *Nature's Metropolis: Chicago And The Great West*
Alfred W. Crosby's *The Columbian Exchange*
Hamid Dabashi's *Iran: A People Interrupted*
David Brion Davis's *The Problem of Slavery in the Age of Revolution*
Nathalie Zemon Davis's *The Return of Martin Guerre*
Jared Diamond's *Guns, Germs & Steel: the Fate of Human Societies*
Frank Dikotter's *Mao's Great Famine*
John W Dower's *War Without Mercy: Race And Power In The Pacific War*
W. E. B. Du Bois's *The Souls of Black Folk*
Richard J. Evans's *In Defence of History*
Lucien Febvre's *The Problem of Unbelief in the 16th Century*
Sheila Fitzpatrick's *Everyday Stalinism*

The Macat Library By Discipline

Eric Foner's *Reconstruction: America's Unfinished Revolution, 1863-1877*
Michel Foucault's *Discipline and Punish*
Michel Foucault's *History of Sexuality*
Francis Fukuyama's *The End of History and the Last Man*
John Lewis Gaddis's *We Now Know: Rethinking Cold War History*
Ernest Gellner's *Nations and Nationalism*
Eugene Genovese's *Roll, Jordan, Roll: The World the Slaves Made*
Carlo Ginzburg's *The Night Battles*
Daniel Goldhagen's *Hitler's Willing Executioners*
Jack Goldstone's *Revolution and Rebellion in the Early Modern World*
Antonio Gramsci's *The Prison Notebooks*
Alexander Hamilton, John Jay & James Madison's *The Federalist Papers*
Christopher Hill's *The World Turned Upside Down*
Carole Hillenbrand's *The Crusades: Islamic Perspectives*
Thomas Hobbes's *Leviathan*
Eric Hobsbawm's *The Age Of Revolution*
John A. Hobson's *Imperialism: A Study*
Albert Hourani's *History of the Arab Peoples*
Samuel P. Huntington's *The Clash of Civilizations and the Remaking of World Order*
C. L. R. James's *The Black Jacobins*
Tony Judt's *Postwar: A History of Europe Since 1945*
Ernst Kantorowicz's *The King's Two Bodies: A Study in Medieval Political Theology*
Paul Kennedy's *The Rise and Fall of the Great Powers*
Ian Kershaw's *The "Hitler Myth": Image and Reality in the Third Reich*
John Maynard Keynes's *The General Theory of Employment, Interest and Money*
Charles P. Kindleberger's *Manias, Panics and Crashes*
Martin Luther King Jr's *Why We Can't Wait*
Henry Kissinger's *World Order: Reflections on the Character of Nations and the Course of History*
Thomas Kuhn's *The Structure of Scientific Revolutions*
Georges Lefebvre's *The Coming of the French Revolution*
John Locke's *Two Treatises of Government*
Niccolò Machiavelli's *The Prince*
Thomas Robert Malthus's *An Essay on the Principle of Population*
Mahmood Mamdani's *Citizen and Subject: Contemporary Africa And The Legacy Of Late
Colonialism*
Karl Marx's *Capital*
Stanley Milgram's *Obedience to Authority*
John Stuart Mill's *On Liberty*
Thomas Paine's *Common Sense*
Thomas Paine's *Rights of Man*
Geoffrey Parker's *Global Crisis: War, Climate Change and Catastrophe in the Seventeenth
Century*
Jonathan Riley-Smith's *The First Crusade and the Idea of Crusading*
Jean-Jacques Rousseau's *The Social Contract*
Joan Wallach Scott's *Gender and the Politics of History*
Theda Skocpol's *States and Social Revolutions*
Adam Smith's *The Wealth of Nations*
Timothy Snyder's *Bloodlands: Europe Between Hitler and Stalin*
Sun Tzu's *The Art of War*
Keith Thomas's *Religion and the Decline of Magic*
Thucydides's *The History of the Peloponnesian War*
Frederick Jackson Turner's *The Significance of the Frontier in American History*
Odd Arne Westad's *The Global Cold War: Third World Interventions And The Making Of Our Times*

LITERATURE

Chinua Achebe's *An Image of Africa: Racism in Conrad's Heart of Darkness*
Roland Barthes's *Mythologies*
Homi K. Bhabha's *The Location of Culture*
Judith Butler's *Gender Trouble*
Simone De Beauvoir's *The Second Sex*
Ferdinand De Saussure's *Course in General Linguistics*
T. S. Eliot's *The Sacred Wood: Essays on Poetry and Criticism*
Zora Neale Huston's *Characteristics of Negro Expression*
Toni Morrison's *Playing in the Dark: Whiteness in the American Literary Imagination*
Edward Said's *Orientalism*
Gayatri Chakravorty Spivak's *Can the Subaltern Speak?*
Mary Wollstonecraft's *A Vindication of the Rights of Women*
Virginia Woolf's *A Room of One's Own*

PHILOSOPHY

Elizabeth Anscombe's *Modern Moral Philosophy*
Hannah Arendt's *The Human Condition*
Aristotle's *Metaphysics*
Aristotle's *Nicomachean Ethics*
Edmund Gettier's *Is Justified True Belief Knowledge?*
Georg Wilhelm Friedrich Hegel's *Phenomenology of Spirit*
David Hume's *Dialogues Concerning Natural Religion*
David Hume's *The Enquiry for Human Understanding*
Immanuel Kant's *Religion within the Boundaries of Mere Reason*
Immanuel Kant's *Critique of Pure Reason*
Søren Kierkegaard's *The Sickness Unto Death*
Søren Kierkegaard's *Fear and Trembling*
C. S. Lewis's *The Abolition of Man*
Alasdair MacIntyre's *After Virtue*
Marcus Aurelius's *Meditations*
Friedrich Nietzsche's *On the Genealogy of Morality*
Friedrich Nietzsche's *Beyond Good and Evil*
Plato's *Republic*
Plato's *Symposium*
Jean-Jacques Rousseau's *The Social Contract*
Gilbert Ryle's *The Concept of Mind*
Baruch Spinoza's *Ethics*
Sun Tzu's *The Art of War*
Ludwig Wittgenstein's *Philosophical Investigations*

POLITICS

Benedict Anderson's *Imagined Communities*
Aristotle's *Politics*
Bernard Bailyn's *The Ideological Origins of the American Revolution*
Edmund Burke's *Reflections on the Revolution in France*
John C. Calhoun's *A Disquisition on Government*
Ha-Joon Chang's *Kicking Away the Ladder*
Hamid Dabashi's *Iran: A People Interrupted*
Hamid Dabashi's *Theology of Discontent: The Ideological Foundation of the Islamic Revolution in Iran*
Robert Dahl's *Democracy and its Critics*
Robert Dahl's *Who Governs?*
David Brion Davis's *The Problem of Slavery in the Age of Revolution*

The Macat Library By Discipline

Alexis De Tocqueville's *Democracy in America*
James Ferguson's *The Anti-Politics Machine*
Frank Dikotter's *Mao's Great Famine*
Sheila Fitzpatrick's *Everyday Stalinism*
Eric Foner's *Reconstruction: America's Unfinished Revolution, 1863-1877*
Milton Friedman's *Capitalism and Freedom*
Francis Fukuyama's *The End of History and the Last Man*
John Lewis Gaddis's *We Now Know: Rethinking Cold War History*
Ernest Gellner's *Nations and Nationalism*
David Graeber's *Debt: the First 5000 Years*
Antonio Gramsci's *The Prison Notebooks*
Alexander Hamilton, John Jay & James Madison's *The Federalist Papers*
Friedrich Hayek's *The Road to Serfdom*
Christopher Hill's *The World Turned Upside Down*
Thomas Hobbes's *Leviathan*
John A. Hobson's *Imperialism: A Study*
Samuel P. Huntington's *The Clash of Civilizations and the Remaking of World Order*
Tony Judt's *Postwar: A History of Europe Since 1945*
David C. Kang's *China Rising: Peace, Power and Order in East Asia*
Paul Kennedy's *The Rise and Fall of Great Powers*
Robert Keohane's *After Hegemony*
Martin Luther King Jr.'s *Why We Can't Wait*
Henry Kissinger's *World Order: Reflections on the Character of Nations and the Course of History*
John Locke's *Two Treatises of Government*
Niccolò Machiavelli's *The Prince*
Thomas Robert Malthus's *An Essay on the Principle of Population*
Mahmood Mamdani's *Citizen and Subject: Contemporary Africa And The Legacy Of Late Colonialism*
Karl Marx's *Capital*
John Stuart Mill's *On Liberty*
John Stuart Mill's *Utilitarianism*
Hans Morgenthau's *Politics Among Nations*
Thomas Paine's *Common Sense*
Thomas Paine's *Rights of Man*
Thomas Piketty's *Capital in the Twenty-First Century*
Robert D. Putnam's *Bowling Alone*
John Rawls's *Theory of Justice*
Jean-Jacques Rousseau's *The Social Contract*
Theda Skocpol's *States and Social Revolutions*
Adam Smith's *The Wealth of Nations*
Sun Tzu's *The Art of War*
Henry David Thoreau's *Civil Disobedience*
Thucydides's *The History of the Peloponnesian War*
Kenneth Waltz's *Theory of International Politics*
Max Weber's *Politics as a Vocation*
Odd Arne Westad's *The Global Cold War: Third World Interventions And The Making Of Our Times*

POSTCOLONIAL STUDIES

Roland Barthes's *Mythologies*
Frantz Fanon's *Black Skin, White Masks*
Homi K. Bhabha's *The Location of Culture*
Gustavo Gutiérrez's *A Theology of Liberation*
Edward Said's *Orientalism*
Gayatri Chakravorty Spivak's *Can the Subaltern Speak?*

PSYCHOLOGY

Gordon Allport's *The Nature of Prejudice*
Alan Baddeley & Graham Hitch's *Aggression: A Social Learning Analysis*
Albert Bandura's *Aggression: A Social Learning Analysis*
Leon Festinger's *A Theory of Cognitive Dissonance*
Sigmund Freud's *The Interpretation of Dreams*
Betty Friedan's *The Feminine Mystique*
Michael R. Gottfredson & Travis Hirschi's *A General Theory of Crime*
Eric Hoffer's *The True Believer: Thoughts on the Nature of Mass Movements*
William James's *Principles of Psychology*
Elizabeth Loftus's *Eyewitness Testimony*
A. H. Maslow's *A Theory of Human Motivation*
Stanley Milgram's *Obedience to Authority*
Steven Pinker's *The Better Angels of Our Nature*
Oliver Sacks's *The Man Who Mistook His Wife For a Hat*
Richard Thaler & Cass Sunstein's *Nudge: Improving Decisions About Health, Wealth and Happiness*
Amos Tversky's *Judgment under Uncertainty: Heuristics and Biases*
Philip Zimbardo's *The Lucifer Effect*

SCIENCE

Rachel Carson's *Silent Spring*
William Cronon's *Nature's Metropolis: Chicago And The Great West*
Alfred W. Crosby's *The Columbian Exchange*
Charles Darwin's *On the Origin of Species*
Richard Dawkin's *The Selfish Gene*
Thomas Kuhn's *The Structure of Scientific Revolutions*
Geoffrey Parker's *Global Crisis: War, Climate Change and Catastrophe in the Seventeenth Century*
Mathis Wackernagel & William Rees's *Our Ecological Footprint*

SOCIOLOGY

Michelle Alexander's *The New Jim Crow: Mass Incarceration in the Age of Colorblindness*
Gordon Allport's *The Nature of Prejudice*
Albert Bandura's *Aggression: A Social Learning Analysis*
Hanna Batatu's *The Old Social Classes And The Revolutionary Movements Of Iraq*
Ha-Joon Chang's *Kicking Away the Ladder*
W. E. B. Du Bois's *The Souls of Black Folk*
Émile Durkheim's *On Suicide*
Frantz Fanon's *Black Skin, White Masks*
Frantz Fanon's *The Wretched of the Earth*
Eric Foner's *Reconstruction: America's Unfinished Revolution, 1863-1877*
Eugene Genovese's *Roll, Jordan, Roll: The World the Slaves Made*
Jack Goldstone's *Revolution and Rebellion in the Early Modern World*
Antonio Gramsci's *The Prison Notebooks*
Richard Herrnstein & Charles A Murray's *The Bell Curve: Intelligence and Class Structure in American Life*
Eric Hoffer's *The True Believer: Thoughts on the Nature of Mass Movements*
Jane Jacobs's *The Death and Life of Great American Cities*
Robert Lucas's *Why Doesn't Capital Flow from Rich to Poor Countries?*
Jay Macleod's *Ain't No Makin' It: Aspirations and Attainment in a Low Income Neighborhood*
Elaine May's *Homeward Bound: American Families in the Cold War Era*
Douglas McGregor's *The Human Side of Enterprise*
C. Wright Mills's *The Sociological Imagination*

Macat Disciplines

Access the greatest ideas and thinkers across entire disciplines, including

Postcolonial Studies

Roland Barthes's *Mythologies*
Frantz Fanon's *Black Skin, White Masks*
Homi K. Bhabha's *The Location of Culture*
Gustavo Gutiérrez's *A Theology of Liberation*
Edward Said's *Orientalism*
Gayatri Chakravorty Spivak's *Can the Subaltern Speak?*

Macat analyses are available from all good bookshops and libraries.

Access hundreds of analyses through one, multimedia tool.
Join free for one month **library.macat.com**

Macat Disciplines

Access the greatest ideas and thinkers across entire disciplines, including

GLOBALIZATION

Arjun Appadurai's, *Modernity at Large: Cultural Dimensions of Globalisation*

James Ferguson's, *The Anti-Politics Machine*

Geert Hofstede's, *Culture's Consequences*

Amartya Sen's, *Development as Freedom*

Macat analyses are available from all good bookshops and libraries.

Access hundreds of analyses through one, multimedia tool.
Join free for one month **library.macat.com**

Macat Pairs

Analyse historical and modern issues from opposite sides of an argument. Pairs include:

HOW TO RUN AN ECONOMY

John Maynard Keynes's
The General Theory OF Employment, Interest and Money

Classical economics suggests that market economies are self-correcting in times of recession or depression, and tend toward full employment and output. But English economist John Maynard Keynes disagrees.

In his ground-breaking 1936 study *The General Theory*, Keynes argues that traditional economics has misunderstood the causes of unemployment. Employment is not determined by the price of labor; it is directly linked to demand. Keynes believes market economies are by nature unstable, and so require government intervention. Spurred on by the social catastrophe of the Great Depression of the 1930s, he sets out to revolutionize the way the world thinks

Milton Friedman's
The Role of Monetary Policy

Friedman's 1968 paper changed the course of economic theory. In just 17 pages, he demolished existing theory and outlined an effective alternate monetary policy designed to secure 'high employment, stable prices and rapid growth.'

Friedman demonstrated that monetary policy plays a vital role in broader economic stability and argued that economists got their monetary policy wrong in the 1950s and 1960s by misunderstanding the relationship between inflation and unemployment. Previous generations of economists had believed that governments could permanently decrease unemployment by permitting inflation—and vice versa. Friedman's most original contribution was to show that this supposed trade-off is an illusion that only works in the short term.

Macat analyses are available from all good bookshops and libraries.

Access hundreds of analyses through one, multimedia tool.
Join free for one month **library.macat.com**

Macat Disciplines

Access the greatest ideas and thinkers across entire disciplines, including

THE FUTURE OF DEMOCRACY

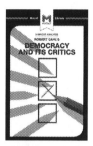

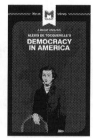

Robert A. Dahl's, *Democracy and Its Critics*
Robert A. Dahl's, *Who Governs?*
Alexis De Toqueville's, *Democracy in America*
Niccolò Machiavelli's, *The Prince*
John Stuart Mill's, *On Liberty*
Robert D. Putnam's, *Bowling Alone*
Jean-Jacques Rousseau's, *The Social Contract*
Henry David Thoreau's, *Civil Disobedience*

Macat analyses are available from all good bookshops and libraries.

Access hundreds of analyses through one, multimedia tool.
Join free for one month **library.macat.com**

Macat Disciplines

Access the greatest ideas and thinkers
across entire disciplines, including

TOTALITARIANISM

Sheila Fitzpatrick's, *Everyday Stalinism*
Ian Kershaw's, *The "Hitler Myth"*
Timothy Snyder's, *Bloodlands*

Macat analyses are available from all good bookshops and libraries.

Access hundreds of analyses through one, multimedia tool.
Join free for one month **library.macat.com**

Macat Pairs

Analyse historical and modern issues from opposite sides of an argument. Pairs include:

RACE AND IDENTITY

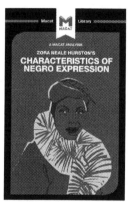

Zora Neale Hurston's
Characteristics of Negro Expression

Using material collected on anthropological expeditions to the South, Zora Neale Hurston explains how expression in African American culture in the early twentieth century departs from the art of white America. At the time, African American art was often criticized for copying white culture. For Hurston, this criticism misunderstood how art works. European tradition views art as something fixed. But Hurston describes a creative process that is alive, ever-changing, and largely improvisational. She maintains that African American art works through a process called 'mimicry'—where an imitated object or verbal pattern, for example, is reshaped and altered until it becomes something new, novel—and worthy of attention.

Frantz Fanon's
Black Skin, White Masks

Black Skin, White Masks offers a radical analysis of the psychological effects of colonization on the colonized.

Fanon witnessed the effects of colonization first hand both in his birthplace, Martinique, and again later in life when he worked as a psychiatrist in another French colony, Algeria. His text is uncompromising in form and argument. He dissects the dehumanizing effects of colonialism, arguing that it destroys the native sense of identity, forcing people to adapt to an alien set of values—including a core belief that they are inferior. This results in deep psychological trauma.

Fanon's work played a pivotal role in the civil rights movements of the 1960s.

Macat analyses are available from all good bookshops and libraries.

Access hundreds of analyses through one, multimedia tool.
Join free for one month **library.macat.com**

Macat Pairs

Analyse historical and modern issues
from opposite sides of an argument.
Pairs include:

INTERNATIONAL RELATIONS IN THE 21ST CENTURY

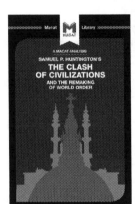

Samuel P. Huntington's
The Clash of Civilisations

In his highly influential 1996 book, Huntington offers a vision of a post-Cold War world in which conflict takes place not between competing ideologies but between cultures. The worst clash, he argues, will be between the Islamic world and the West: the West's arrogance and belief that its culture is a "gift" to the world will come into conflict with Islam's obstinacy and concern that its culture is under attack from a morally decadent "other."

Clash inspired much debate between different political schools of thought. But its greatest impact came in helping define American foreign policy in the wake of the 2001 terrorist attacks in New York and Washington.

Francis Fukuyama's
The End of History and the Last Man

Published in 1992, *The End of History and the Last Man* argues that capitalist democracy is the final destination for all societies. Fukuyama believed democracy triumphed during the Cold War because it lacks the "fundamental contradictions" inherent in communism and satisfies our yearning for freedom and equality. Democracy therefore marks the endpoint in the evolution of ideology, and so the "end of history." There will still be "events," but no fundamental change in ideology.

Macat analyses are available from all good bookshops and libraries.

Access hundreds of analyses through one, multimedia tool.
Join free for one month **library.macat.com**

Macat Disciplines

Access the greatest ideas and thinkers across entire disciplines, including

MAN AND THE ENVIRONMENT

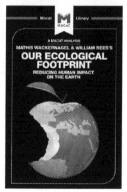

The Brundtland Report's, *Our Common Future*
Rachel Carson's, *Silent Spring*
James Lovelock's, *Gaia: A New Look at Life on Earth*
Mathis Wackernagel & William Rees's, *Our Ecological Footprint*

Macat analyses are available from all good bookshops and libraries.

Access hundreds of analyses through one, multimedia tool.
Join free for one month **library.macat.com**

Printed in the United States
by Baker & Taylor Publisher Services